*Arthur Miller's*

# Death of a Salesman

*Text by*
**Nick A. Yasinski**
*(M.A., Rutgers University)*

*Illustrations by*
**Karen Pica**

*Research & Education Association*
**Dr. M. Fogiel, Director**

**MAXnotes**® for
DEATH OF A SALESMAN

Printed in the United States of America


Library of Congress Control Number 2001086588

International Standard Book Number 0-87891-995-3


**MAXnotes**® is a registered trademark of Research & Education Association, Piscataway, New Jersey 08854

# What **MAXnotes**® Will Do for You

This book is intended to help you absorb the essential contents and features of Arthur Miller's *Death of a Salesman* and to help you gain a thorough understanding of the work. Our book has been designed to do this more quickly and effectively than any other study guide.

For best results, this **MAXnotes** book should be used as a companion to the actual work, not instead of it. The interaction between the two will greatly benefit you.

To help you in your studies, this book presents the most up-to-date interpretations of every section of the actual work, followed by questions and fully explained answers that will enable you to analyze the material critically. The questions also will help you to test your understanding of the work and will prepare you for discussions and exams.

Meaningful illustrations are included to further enhance your understanding and enjoyment of the literary work. The illustrations are designed to place you into the mood and spirit of the work's settings.

The **MAXnotes** also include summaries, character lists, explanations of plot, and section-by-section analyses. A biography of the author and discussion of the work's historical context will help you put this literary piece into the proper framework of what is taking place.

The use of this study guide will save you the hours of preparation time that would ordinarily be required to arrive at a complete grasp of this work of literature. You will be well-prepared for classroom discussions, homework, and exams. The guidelines that are included for writing papers and reports on various topics will prepare you for any added work which may be assigned.

The **MAXnotes** will take your grades "to the max."

Dr. Max Fogiel
Program Director

# Contents

**Section One: *Introduction*** ............................................... 1

   The Life and Work of Arthur Miller ................................. 1

   Historical Background ....................................................... 3

   Master List of Characters .................................................. 5

   Summary of the Play ......................................................... 6

   Estimated Reading Time .................................................... 8

> **Each part includes List of Characters, Summary, Analysis, Study Questions and Answers, and Suggested Essay Topics.**

**Section Two: *Act I*** .......................................................... 9

   Part 1 ................................................................................. 9

   Part 2 ............................................................................... 16

   Part 3 ............................................................................... 22

   Part 4 ............................................................................... 32

**Section Three: *Act II*** ................................................... 41

   Part 1 ............................................................................... 41

   Part 2 ............................................................................... 49

   Part 3 ............................................................................... 56

   Part 4 ............................................................................... 62

   Part 5 ............................................................................... 69

Part 6 .................................................................. 76

**Section Four:** *Requiem* ...................................... 85

**Section Five:** *Sample Analytical Paper Topics* .................. 92

**Section Six:** *Bibliography* .................................... 96

## *MAXnotes® are simply the best – but don't just take our word for it...*

"... I have told every bookstore in the area to carry your MAXnotes. They are the only notes I recommend to my students. There is no comparison between MAXnotes and all other notes ..."
  – *High School Teacher & Reading Specialist,*
  *Arlington High School, Arlington, MA*

"... I discovered the MAXnotes when a friend loaned me her copy of the *MAXnotes for Romeo and Juliet*. The book really helped me understand the story. Please send me a list of stores in my area that carry the MAXnotes. I would like to use more of them ..."
  – *Student, San Marino, CA*

"... The two MAXnotes titles that I have used have been very, very useful in helping me understand the subject matter reviewed. Thank you for creating the MAXnotes series ..."
  – *Student, Morrisville, PA*

# A Glance at Some of the Characters

Willy

Linda

Biff

Happy

Ben

Charley

Bernard

Howard

# SECTION ONE

# *Introduction*

### *The Life and Work of Arthur Miller*

Arthur Miller was born October 17, 1915, in New York City, to Isadore and Augusta Barnett Miller. He grew up with an older brother and a younger sister and received his earliest schooling in Harlem in the 1920s. His middle-class family fell upon difficult times when his father's clothing business experienced devastating economic damage, forcing the family to move to Brooklyn shortly before the Depression.

At Abraham Lincoln High School in Brooklyn, Miller was more an athlete than a scholar; an average student, he did not read much literature, preferring instead boys' adventure stories. Because his parents could not afford to send him to college when he graduated high school in 1932 (in the middle of the Depression), he worked at several jobs, including one at an auto parts warehouse and one as a radio singer. He saved enough money during this time to enter school at the University of Michigan, where he had applied earlier but was rejected.

In college, his growing interest in literature led him to write a number of successful plays as an undergraduate. For two of them, *No Villain* (1936) and *Honors at Dawn* (1937), he received the University of Michigan's prestigious Hopwood Award. After graduating from Michigan, Miller married Mary Grace Slattery in 1940, worked briefly for the Federal Theatre Project (the Depression-era government agency that paid young writers for their work), and wrote short radio scripts.

In 1944, during World War II, Miller traveled to several army bases in the U.S. as a researcher for the 1945 film *Story of G.I. Joe*. Miller published his observations in *Situation Normal*, describing one soldier's feelings after returning from war. The account reveals Miller's distrust of the easy and blind patriotism that he thought characterized popular literature and film in America. Miller's desire to question the motives behind conventional sentimentality toward war comes through in *Death of a Salesman* as well, where the American dream seems to lose its innocent veneer.

Miller's most successful Broadway plays have been *Death of a Salesman* (1949), which won the Pulitzer Prize and the New York Drama Critics Circle Award, and *The Crucible* (1953). *The Crucible* – set during the seventeenth-century witch trials of Salem, Massachusetts – was a pointed criticism of the then-current "witch-hunt" that U.S. Senator Joseph McCarthy led against American politicians and public figures thought to be associated with Communism. At that time (the 1950s), the U.S. was in the middle of the Cold War, an ideological battle with the Soviet Union. Historians have roundly condemned the frenzy with which McCarthy and others sought to attack, often with no foundation, Americans interested in communism, socialism, or significant socioeconomic change. Miller himself was called before the hearings of the House Committee on Un-American Activities and convicted of contempt of Congress when, stating he was not himself a Communist, he refused to name people he had met at a Communist writers meeting. The conviction was later overturned on a technicality.

Associated with politically left causes and organizations throughout his career, Miller did not always reflect his political concerns directly in his writings. Like Henrik Ibsen, the late nineteenth-century Norwegian playwright whom he admired, Miller tended toward realism in his style. Miller's realism, though, was a social and psychological realism that took advantage of time-shifts, memories, and innovative set design to articulate characters' complex relations to their social, economic, religious, familial, and gender roles. In addition to *Death of a Salesman* and *The Crucible*, Miller's most notable plays included *All My Sons* (1947), *An Enemy of the People* (1950, adapted from Ibsen), *A View from the Bridge* (1956), *After the Fall* (1964), *Incident at Vichy* (1964), *The Price*

(1968), *The Creation of the World and Other Business* (1972), *The Archbishop's Ceiling* (1977), and *The American Clock* (1980). He also wrote *Focus*, a novel about anti-Semitism, a topic that greatly occupied Miller and that informed both *Incident at Vichy* and his television screenplay *Playing for Time* (1980). Miller's autobiography, *Timebends: A Life* (1987), and *The Theater Essays of Arthur Miller* (1978) give insight into his life and his theories on drama. His works have enjoyed several new stage, film, and television productions over the years and are consistently produced by small theaters around the country.

Miller and his wife Mary Grace Slattery divorced in 1955, and in 1956, Miller married movie star Marilyn Monroe. Because of both Miller and Monroe's fame at that time, the marriage received enormous publicity. The two celebrities divorced in 1961, and in 1962 Miller married photographer Ingeborg Morath, with whom he continues to live in Connecticut.

### Historical Background

Miller tells the reader at the outset of the play that *Death of a Salesman* takes place "in the New York and Boston of today." When the play opened, "today" meant 1949, a moment in American history when many people – riding an economy rescued from the Great Depression of the 1930s by the domestic industrial boom of World War II (1939-45) – found a more prosperous life within reach. In the late 1940s and throughout the 1950s, many pursued "the American dream" of hard work rewarded by middle-class signs of success such as a house, a car, a college education, and household appliances. The dream held the possibility for greater personal wealth, even while African-Americans, Hispanic-Americans, Asian-Americans, Native Americans, and new immigrants struggled to gain the civil rights that would give them equal opportunity to chase that dream. *Death of a Salesman* has frequently been understood as a commentary on the American dream and whether (1) the dream's economic prosperity is truly available to anyone who works diligently, and (2) the importance the dream places on material wealth invites selfishness and social injustice.

By 1949, World War II was over, Harry Truman was president of the United States, and the U.S. had not yet begun its involvement in the Korean War (1950-53). The Cold War with the Soviet Union brought a nuclear arms race as the U.S., a victor of World War II, asserted its role as not only a political and military world power but as an overwhelming international cultural force. American movies and manufactured goods were exported along with the American dream and American capitalism. By the end of the 1940s, Americans earned an average of 15 times the yearly wage of the rest of the world, a fact that reveals the overall wealth of the U.S., albeit a wealth that was extracted from but not shared with the working-class people in the U.S. and foreign countries. Despite the looming possibility of nuclear war and, for many, the often elusive "better life," Americans' optimism dominated public discourse with, as Miller's play suggests, a buoyancy comparable to loyalty to one's favorite sports team.

Although television had been invented before the end of the 1940s, it did not fully surpass radio in prominence and audience size until several years later. And while traveling salesmen are rare in the 1990s, they were common in the 1940s, selling items such as brushes and vacuum cleaners door-to-door. Social relations were also different from today. Linda Loman's role as a loyal and often shy housewife and mother does not necessarily represent all women's lives in the 1940s, nor does Miller necessarily approve of the role. However, her behavior does suggest the cultural notions, common in that period, of restrained, even timid, femininity; and, as the play bears out, masculinity of the time was overly identified with the virile figures of the athlete, businessman, and soldier.

*Death of a Salesman* opened on Broadway at the Morosco Theatre on February 10, 1949 and ran for more than two years, tallying 742 performances. Its initial success has been reinforced by several regional, repertory, and touring productions over the years. One of its most famous productions was in Beijing, China, during a time (1983) when the U.S. and China were staunch ideological opponents. The play's most recent notable revival starred Dustin Hoffman as Willy Loman in 1984. While reading *Death of a Salesman*, the reader should remember that it is not a novel, but a play meant for the stage. As such, the play asks the audience to notice not just what is being said by characters, but what music, costumes, set design, and unheard actions contribute to the overall effect.

The general public has continually come out to see *Death of a Salesman* in significant numbers, drawn to the pathos of its central character, Willy Loman, whom audiences tend to regard as a symbol of the ordinary American. Although the play appears to pose as one of its central questions how much sympathy Willy deserves, Miller himself has endorsed the idea that the play is a tragedy in the true dramatic sense of the word – a tragedy of the common man, the "low man." As this historical background sketch has shown, *Death of a Salesman* owes much to its historical moment; nevertheless, the idea of a tragedy of the common man imbues the play with a sense of timelessness – even if that quality might eventually be linked to a particularly American, post-World War II way of thinking.

Some critics and academics have not liked *Death of a Salesman* and dispute its status as a viable tragedy. They argue that Willy is not a compelling protagonist but merely a pitiful man, a loudmouth and cheat. Compared with the other two most prominent mid-twentieth-century American playwrights – Eugene O'Neill and Tennessee Williams – Miller's plays in the tradition of socially and politically conscious realism usually do not achieve the formal, Expressionist innovation of his predecessor O'Neill or the poetic writing of his contemporary Williams. Nonetheless, *Death of a Salesman* possesses enough of both styles to have earned praise for its innovative stage orchestration of space and memory, as well as its several captivating speeches, at once earnest and self-deceiving.

### *Master List of Characters*

**Willy Loman** – *The "salesman" of the play's title.*

**Linda Loman** – *Wife of Willy, mother of Biff and Happy.*

**Biff Loman** – *Elder son of Willy and Linda.*

**Happy Loman** – *Younger son of Willy and Linda, often simply called Hap.*

**Ben Loman** – *Willy's older brother (Biff and Happy's uncle). He made his fortune in African diamonds as a very young man.*

**Charley** – *Neighbor of the Lomans. He is called Uncle Charley by Biff and Happy, even though he is not their actual uncle.*

**Bernard** – *Charley's son, who helps Biff with his homework and whom Willy, Biff, and Happy tease for being an unmanly bookworm.*

**Howard Wagner** – *Willy's boss, who is younger than Willy. Howard's father had been Willy's boss until his death.*

**The Woman** – *The woman with whom Willy has an extramarital affair during his sales trips to Boston.*

**Miss Forsythe** – *A woman whom Biff and Happy meet in the restaurant. (She is referred to as simply "Girl" in the play before her name is given.)*

**Letta** – *Miss Forsythe's friend. She eventually joins Miss Forsythe, Willy, Biff, and Happy at the restaurant.*

**Stanley** – *A young waiter at the restaurant where Biff, Happy, and Willy meet in Act II.*

**Jenny** – *Charley's secretary.*

### Summary of the Play

Arthur Miller did not divide his play into scenes within each act. Instead, the action is continuous, even when flashbacks occur. Therefore, for the purposes of this study guide, the acts have been divided into parts, each covering about 15 pages of the play.

*Death of a Salesman* is subtitled "Certain Private Conversations in Two Acts and a Requiem" and, accordingly, the acts are divided into conversations – in the present and from the past – that flow in and out of each other. The play encompasses an evening and the following day, but the action is interrupted by or mixed with flashbacks or memories of a period approximately 17 years earlier.

Act I opens in Willy Loman's house in Brooklyn. Willy, a traveling salesman of 63, is exhausted after years of making his trips. (Even by the end of the play, we do not know what product he sells.) He has yet to reach a level of success that would allow him to stop traveling and afford the household bills that always seem to swallow his diminishing wages. We learn that Willy's grown son, Biff, has returned to visit. And we come to know Willy's character as he

complains to his wife Linda about his disappointment in Biff's failure to find a steady, serious job. Willy is tired, confused, and argu-
mentative, a man who loves his son and has tried to infuse him
with a salesman's enthusiastic optimism and self-confidence.

In the rest of Act I, through various flashbacks that might also
be Willy's memories, we become familiar with the salesman's philosophy of success that has guided Willy to his current less-than-
successful state. Compared with his neighbor Charley and Charley's
son Bernard, Willy and his sons Biff and Hap are athletic, rather
than studious; in Willy's mind, a likable personality is more important for success than academic grades. Willy endorses Biff's cheating at school; and, we learn, Willy himself cheated on his wife by
having an extramarital affair with a woman in Boston. Linda in-
forms Biff and Hap she has discovered that Willy has secretly started
to contemplate suicide. The evening of Act I winds down as Biff
and Hap attempt to cheer up Willy by promising to go into business together.

In Act II, which encompasses the day following the evening of
Act I, Willy asks his boss for a new, non-traveling job. Instead of
being rewarded for years of service, Willy is fired because he has
not been able to sell enough. Bewildered, he asks his friend Charley
for another of many loans and, while doing so, meets Bernard, now
a successful lawyer. In the evening, Willy joins Biff and Hap at a
restaurant and eventually tells them his bad news; unable to de-
press a father who wants good news at the end of a terrible day,
Biff fails to tell Willy that he did not get the loan that would have
made it possible for Hap and him to start a business together. The
scene then changes to years earlier, when Biff comes to Boston just
after flunking math, which has endangered his chances for college
by preventing him from graduating high school. Biff there discovers Willy is having an affair.

In the present, when Biff and Hap return to the house, their
mother reproaches them for abandoning Willy in the restaurant.
Delusional, Willy is planting a garden in the dark and having an
imaginary conversation with his elder brother Ben, who made a
fortune in diamonds as a young man. Biff tries to explain the
ungranted loan to Willy, as well as his decision to leave so as not to
disappoint Willy ever again. Willy believes Biff has been unsuccess-

ful out of spite for him, but when Biff begins to cry, Willy sees Biff's love for him. Inspired by this realization, but obviously disoriented, Willy sneaks away that night and kills himself in a car accident, thinking his life insurance money will give Biff a new start and that a well-attended funeral will prove his own popularity. In a very short third act that Miller calls a "Requiem," we see that almost no one has attended the funeral. Although Hap defends Willy's "good dream," Biff is subdued and Linda weeps as she asks Willy's grave why he did such a thing.

### Estimated Reading Time

The entire play is about 130 pages, but because of the spaces between characters' lines it will read faster than a novel. An average student, reading about 25-30 pages an hour, will need 4-5 hours to read the play. If you do not have enough time to read it all at once, the best plan might be two sittings – Act I, then Act II and the short "Requiem" – of about two hours each.

# SECTION TWO

# *Act I*

## Act I, Part 1

New Characters:

**Willy Loman:** *Linda's husband, Biff and Happy's father; the "salesman" of the play's title*

**Linda:** *wife of Willy, mother of Biff and Happy*

**Biff:** *elder son of Willy and Linda*

**Happy:** *younger son of Willy and Linda, often simply called Hap*

### *Summary*

Part 1 covers the author's pre-play description of the set, as well as the opening action until Linda says, "Be careful on the stairs, dear!"

Even before the characters appear on stage, the audience sees the set design. Miller's description of the set is important as it establishes the tone of the play. The set shows both the inside and outside of Willy Loman's humble house in New York City; the time is present day, which was 1949 when *Death of a Salesman* first opened. A "fragile-seeming" house, it is hedged in, surrounded by recently erected apartment buildings. Blue light falls on the house, giving it "an air of the dream," while "an angry glow of orange" colors the edges of the set.

The kitchen occupies center stage, flanked by a bedroom at a

raised level on the right. Behind and above the kitchen is another bedroom, and a doorway draped with a curtain leads out from the back of the kitchen to an unseen living room. The setting is completely or, in places, partially transparent. Miller tells the reader that when the characters are in the present, the actors will respect the "walls" of the house and enter only through doors; in the scenes from the past, however, the actors will enter or exit by walking *through* the transparent walls.

Flute music reminiscent of "grass and trees and the horizon" plays as "the Salesman," Willy Loman, enters the house at night time. A tired-looking man in his sixties, Willy has returned home early from a business sales trip he began that morning. His wife Linda wonders why Willy has returned unexpectedly, and Willy responds that while driving he had begun daydreaming and almost had an accident. Willy is frightened at his own loss of control, but also disappointed that he, his company's "New England man," will not make his business meeting in Portland, Maine, tomorrow. "I could sell them!" he tells Linda. Willy is convinced, and Linda agrees, that after years as a loyal traveling salesman he should be rewarded with a non-traveling position at the company office in New York; we do not learn what Willy sells, although we see his sample cases.

Willy and Linda's 34-year-old son Biff has returned to visit his parents, but when Linda brings up the fact that Biff and their other son (Happy) went on a date earlier that evening, Willy begins finding fault with Biff. Willy and Biff have been at odds with each other for a long time. Willy cannot understand why Biff, since high school, has needed to "find himself" by working menial odd jobs, the latest being a job as a farmhand out West. Willy questions how, with such "personal attractiveness," Biff has gotten lost "in the greatest country in the world." Willy's mood, however, quickly changes. Convinced that "Biff is a lazy bum," Willy then remembers how proud he was of Biff's popularity in high school and says, "There's one thing about Biff – he's not lazy."

Reassured that Biff will find a successful career, Willy begins expressing his frustration with how their house and suburban neighborhood have suffered the encroachment of people and large buildings from the city. Willy finally heads down to the kitchen from

the bedroom to make a sandwich. Adding to his existing confusion is his realization that moments ago he thought that today he had driven a different, older car than the one he actually drove. Lying in their bedroom above the kitchen, Biff and Happy do not hear their parents discussing Biff but do begin listening shortly before Willy goes to the kitchen.

### Analysis

The set design of *Death of a Salesman* was innovative when the play was first produced in 1949, since it allowed Miller's characters to move between present and past, the real and the imaginary, without cumbersome set changes. Moreover, the set design helps Miller suggest the way the characters, especially Willy, live in the past as much as the present.

The blue light around the set, indicating "an air of the dream," corresponds to Willy's self-confidence ("I could sell them!") in the face of what are intimidating, depressing circumstances. Simultaneously, "an air of the dream" might refer to all the characters' anxious, dazed sense of being lost. The large apartment buildings are crowding Willy and Linda, beating down on them the same way many unrewarding years as a traveling salesman have weighed on Willy. Willy's optimism in his ability to sell and later in Biff's eventual success reveals a salesman's belief that the present is never as bad as it seems and that the future will always be even better. For many people, that optimism also connotes an enthusiasm for self-improvement associated with the American dream. What place "personal attractiveness" like Biff's has in the American dream, though, is debatable. The upward mobility of the American dream has usually been identified with hard work, not personality, but – at least to someone like Willy – sometimes honest effort has not seemed as important as who you know or who likes you.

When Willy becomes angry with Biff, then quickly regains confidence in him, the reader must begin to wonder whether Willy isn't merely exhausted but prone to fooling himself. Is Willy really a good salesman? Is Biff a bum or not? Is success measured only by a lucrative career? Although Linda consoles Willy, the reader must also wonder if she suspects him of self-deception. Miller's notes at the beginning of the play describe Linda as follows:

...she more than loves [Willy], she admires him, as though his mercurial nature, his temper, his massive dreams and little cruelties, served her only as sharp reminders of the turbulent longings within him, longings which she shares but lacks the temperament to utter and follow to their end.

The description and Linda's sympathetic behavior cast her as a faithful wife. Her traditional role reflects the conservatism of American culture at the time, as well as the difficult life she has shared with Willy.

As the play progresses, the reader should question whether any characters are more truthful or honestly perceptive than other characters. Look for the ways in which exaggerations and untruths are mixed with more accurate observations until recognizing "reality" becomes a very confusing matter.

### Study Questions

1. In what city does Willy Loman live?

2. What surrounds Willy's house?

3. In what way has Miller used transparent walls to indicate when characters are in the past rather than the present?

4. What is Willy's job?

5. From where has Willy returned early? Why?

6. Does Willy have confidence in his ability to do his own job?

7. Who has come home to visit Willy and Linda?

8. Whom does Willy criticize and why?

9. Why does Willy stop his criticizing?

10. Who begins to listen to Willy and Linda's conversation just before Willy goes to the kitchen to make a sandwich?

### Answers

1. Willy Loman lives in New York City.

2. Recently built apartment buildings surround the house, giving it a small, fragile appearance.

3. When action occurs in the past, characters enter or exit through the walls. When action occurs in the present, they enter and exit through the doors.

4. He is a traveling salesman; specifically, he is his company's salesman for New England.

5. He has returned early from a sales trip to New England after almost having a car accident while driving.

6. Yes. His confidence is evident in his remark to Linda: "I could sell them!" However, Willy does seem worried or scared about his daydreaming and the loss of self-control it implies.

7. Their son, Biff, has come to visit them.

8. Willy criticizes Biff because, at the age of 34, Biff does not have a successful career. Willy does not approve of Biff's many years of insignificant jobs.

9. Willy stops criticizing Biff when Willy remembers Biff's high school popularity and athleticism. Willy's mood shifts and he starts to think Biff will eventually have a promising career as an adult.

10. Biff and Happy, awake in their upstairs bedroom, hear their parents talking toward the end of their conversation.

### Suggested Essay Topics

1. In this opening section we meet Willy Loman. Examine his personality and character. What influences have shaped his view of his job, his family, and the world in general? What is responsible for his tendency to change temperament quickly? What contradictions in behavior does he exhibit?

2. How does the playwright communicate Willy's outlook and emotions to the reader or audience not only through Willy's words but through his appearance, Linda's reactions, the set design, and other means?

# Act I, Part 2

New Character:

**Bernard:** *meek, younger acquaintance of Biff and Happy who helps Biff study math*

## *Summary*

Part 2 covers the action up to Willy's line, "Good work, Biff."

After Willy has wandered into the living room, where although unseen, he can occasionally be heard talking to himself, the scene shifts to Biff and Happy, talking to each other in their childhood bedroom. Biff is now 34, two years older than Hap. Hap tells Biff he is worried about their father's absent-mindedness, but the conversation quickly turns to reminiscences about the brothers' youthful sexual prowess with women. Biff moves their discussion back to the subject of their father, prompting Hap to reveal that it is Biff's general unsettledness and lack of career to which Willy constantly returns when talking to himself. Biff tries to explain to Hap that he could not bear slowly working his way up in a career as a salesman or shipping clerk, but that neither has his latest job as a farmhand in Texas given him any sense of a stable future. Biff says, "Maybe I oughta get stuck into something. Maybe that's my trouble. I'm like a boy. I'm not married, I'm not in business, I just – I'm like a boy."

Hap, whose low-level job is the kind Biff has fled, admits that he, too, is lonely and bored, despite a decent salary and the possibility for eventual promotion. Biff suggests they escape their present situations and buy a farm out West. Hap declines the offer and states, "I gotta show some of those pompous, self-important executives over there that Hap Loman can make the grade." Boredom and an empty sense of competition, he confesses, have contributed to a series of unsatisfying affairs with the girlfriends of executives in his company. Acknowledging his dishonesty, as well as the pleasure he derives from it, he likens his behavior to his inability to refrain from accepting bribes at work. Before the brothers fall asleep again, Biff announces that he intends to ask for a loan from Bill Oliver, for whom he worked years ago; Biff wonders for a moment, though, whether Oliver will remember or ever knew

that Biff stole a carton of basketballs from him.

Biff and Hap hear Willy mumbling to himself downstairs as they go back to sleep. On stage, the light fades away from the brothers and focuses on Willy in the kitchen. The set changes to let the audience know a flashback is occurring: the surrounding apartment buildings disappear, green leaves appear, and cheerful music plays. Willy seems to speak to Biff and Hap, but no one is visible. Eventually, Biff and Hap enter as teenagers. Biff wears a sweater with a large "S" and carries a football; Hap carries the pail and rags that the boys have just used to wash the car. Willy, just returned from a sales trip, is in good spirits and gives his sons a punching bag as a gift. Biff, we learn, has borrowed the football from school without the coach's permission. Without scolding him, Willy tells him to return it and proceeds in his enthusiastic mood to tell Biff and Hap of his great success and popularity as a salesman.

The conversation is interrupted when the young Bernard enters, dressed in knickers, to tell Biff he should be studying with him today. After he warns Biff that flunking the upcoming test will prevent him from graduating high school, Willy tells Biff to go study. Before Biff goes, Willy dismisses Bernard as an "anemic," and, scoffing at his timidity and studiousness, remarks to his own sons that "the man who makes an appearance in the business world, the man who creates personal interest, is the man who gets ahead."

### Analysis

This segment of the play works in a reverse order of sorts: the audience listens to the bedroom conversation between Biff and Hap and then through the flashback sees the childhood that led the brothers to their present states in life. In the stage directions to the bedroom conversation, Miller tells the reader that both men are athletically built, but Biff "bears a worn air." Happy, like Biff, is "lost" but in a different way. Hap seems more content, less defeated, and "sexuality is like a visible color on him."

As Biff recounts his dissatisfaction with mundane office jobs, the reader feels some sympathy with him; perhaps Willy's frustration with Biff is in fact unreasonable. That sympathy becomes more complicated, however, as we learn that Biff has not been able or willing to hold *any* job, and that he intends to request a loan from

a man from whom he once stole. Although Hap, too, seems very likable at first – a simple, happy person as his name would indicate – we begin to doubt his integrity, as well. His unwillingness to stop preying on the fiancees and girlfriends of his bosses and to quit taking bribes suggests how he possesses a hollow competitiveness; that competitive drive will lead not to his fulfillment but merely to a need to grasp for more unrewarding, short-lived pleasures. Despite their questionable behavior, though, Biff and Hap manage to convince themselves and, perhaps, the audience, that change may be possible, and that their flaws are not insurmountable.

Miller orchestrates the flashback to Biff and Hap's teenage years through Willy's delusional ramblings in the kitchen. Willy talks himself and the audience right back into the past, which is confirmed when we see the young Biff and Hap. This whole flashback episode, then, may be a figment of Willy's imagination. In the episode, we see the Loman family during happier days. Willy loves his sons and they adore him. Willy's confidence in himself as a salesman and in the future success of his sons, however, cannot help but strike the reader as a little pretentious, as well as unfounded.

Willy likes to talk, especially about himself, and places more importance on "appearance" and personality than honesty and studying. For Willy, "success" is connected to a particular type of athletic, virile manhood, one represented by his sons' interest in football and boxing. When Willy calls Bernard an "anemic" and says he is "liked but not well liked," Willy mocks Bernard for being unmanly. Miller tells us that Bernard is "earnest and loyal, a worried boy"; we must reconsider the wisdom of Willy's disapproval of Bernard, though, once we remember how Biff and Happy have not necessarily met their father's standard of "success" as adults. After seeing this flashback, the audience must wonder about the Lomans' less-than-pleasant circumstances in the present: Have Willy, Biff, and Hap been unlucky, or can they blame only themselves for their growing disillusionment? Is there a middle ground between those two possibilities?

### Study Questions

1.  How old are Biff and Hap during their conversation in the

bedroom? Does that conversation take place in the past or the present?

2. What was Biff's latest job? What kind of job or career can he not bear?

3. Why doesn't Hap accept Biff's invitation to go West to start a farm?

4. In what kind of unethical behavior has Hap engaged?

5. What plan does Biff tell Hap about as the brothers fall back asleep? Why is Biff somewhat nervous about the plan?

6. How does the audience know that a flashback occurs?

7. Is Willy bashful or shy about his ability as a salesman?

8. How are Biff and Hap different from Bernard?

9. According to Willy, what makes someone successful?

10. How might the flashback affect what you think of the Biff and Hap in the present?

### Answers

1. The conversation takes place in the present, when Biff is 34 and Hap is 32.

2. Biff's latest job was as a farmhand in Texas. He cannot bear the drudgery and slow advancement involved with jobs such as a salesman and a shipping clerk.

3. Hap refuses to go because he wants to "show some of those pompous, self-important executives over there that Hap Loman can make the grade."

4. He has slept with the girlfriends of his bosses and has accepted bribes.

5. Biff tells Hap he intends to ask for a loan from Bill Oliver; Biff is slightly nervous, though, because he once stole a carton of basketballs from Oliver.

6. Miller indicates that a flashback is occurring by having the surrounding apartment buildings disappear, green leaves appear, and cheerful music begin to play. We know for cer-

tain that we are in the past when Biff and Hap appear as teenagers rather than adults.

7.  No. Willy tells his sons at length how popular and successful
    he is as a salesman.

8.  Biff and Hap are athletic and outgoing, while Bernard is stu-
    dious, earnest, and worried. Willy thinks Bernard is "anemic"
    and unmasculine.

9.  According to Willy, the athletic and outgoing character of his
    sons, rather than the timidity of Bernard, will make a per-
    son "well liked" and thus successful. In Willy's eyes, "the man
    who makes an appearance in the business world, the man
    who creates personal interest, is the man who gets ahead."

10. Because the flashback shows Biff and Hap during a happy
    period of their lives, the audience may tend to feel sorry for
    the problems they endure in the present. On the other hand,
    the flashback suggests the way Biff and Hap's dissatisfaction
    with their lives in the present may derive in part from the
    beliefs Willy instilled in them as children.

### Suggested Essay Topics

1.  Examine how Biff and Hap's adult lives show the influence
    of their childhood as seen in the flashback.

2.  Write an essay that discusses the way in which Willy equates
    "success" and conventional notions of masculinity. Has that
    equation proved valid for Biff and Hap?

# Act I, Part 3

New Characters:

**Charley:** *neighbor of the Lomans, called Uncle Charley by Biff and
Happy, even though he is not their actual uncle; father of Bernard*

**Ben**: *Willy's older brother (Biff and Happy's uncle); made his fortune in African diamonds as a very young man*

**The Woman**: *the woman with whom Willy has an extramarital affair during his sales trips to Boston*

### Summary

Part 3 covers the action up to Willy's line "...I was right! I was right! I was right!"

As the previous section ends, we remain in the flashback. Willy and Linda are alone, discussing the outcome of Willy's sales trip and whether there is enough money to pay the bills. Willy exaggerates his success, but is slowly forced to admit his trip was not very profitable once Linda begins listing the household expenses. Trying to keep his own spirits up, as well as Linda's, Willy insists, "Oh, I'll knock 'em dead next week. I'll go to Hartford. I'm very well liked in Hartford. You know, the trouble is, Linda, people don't seem to take to me." Willy's optimism falters uncharacteristically, and the audience sees his desperation as he tells Linda that he fears people see him as fat, foolish, and too talkative.

Linda comforts her husband, reassuring him that he's "the handsomest man in the world" and idolized by his sons. Willy replies earnestly, "You're the best there is, Linda, you're a pal, you know that? On the road – on the road I want to grab you sometimes and just kiss the life outa you." As Willy finishes these loving words, he appears to daydream. On the left part of the stage, a woman appears silhouetted and then standing in front of a mirror as she dresses. From the conversation between Willy and this woman (whose name we do not learn), the audience can surmise she is Willy's mistress in Boston. After Willy kisses her, and after she thanks him for a gift of new stockings, the woman's laughter fades away; the woman is gone again – Willy's daydream memory is over.

Willy wakes from this daze and chastises Linda for mending her stockings; as Bernard runs by, Willy demands he give Biff the answers for the upcoming test. Willy's temper builds as Bernard and Linda begin to speak: Bernard cannot cheat for Biff on this test, Linda wants Biff to return the borrowed football, Bernard says

Biff is driving without a license, Linda says Biff is too rough with girls. As the woman's laugh rises in the background, Willy becomes overwhelmed, yelling "Shut up!" Bernard backs out of the room and Linda leaves almost crying as the flashback ends and Willy is left alone in the kitchen, where he originally came to make a sandwich.

Hap comes downstairs to help his father to bed but leaves when Charley appears and begins to play a late-night game of cards with Willy. Charley – "a large man, slow of speech, laconic, immovable" – engages in teasing banter with Willy, who feels insulted when Charley good-heartedly offers Willy a job. Charley urges Willy not to worry about Biff, but Willy is not soothed and begins talking aloud to his older brother, Ben, visible only to Willy and the audience. Charley and Willy continue playing cards, but half of Willy's comments are directed toward Ben – "a stolid man, in his sixties, with a mustache and an authoritative air" – who made his fortune in African diamonds as a very young man. Charley quits the game after Willy accuses him of cheating, and the scene slips into a full flashback as Willy walks through a wall-line to shake Ben's hand.

The flashback shows the audience the first time Willy and his family met Ben, years ago when Biff and Hap were teenagers. Willy did not know Ben or their father while growing up and thus asks Ben to tell Biff and Hap about their grandfather. "With one gadget," Ben says of his and Willy's father, "he made more in a week than a man like you could make in a lifetime." Willy admires Ben tremendously and vigorously seeks his approval for the way he has raised Biff and Hap. Bragging about his sons' resourcefulness, Willy tells Ben how Biff and Hap bring home lumber and other materials to help Willy with home repair projects. Shortly after Willy sends Biff and Hap to get some sand from a nearby construction site, Bernard enters to warn Willy and Linda that a watchman is chasing Biff and Hap after again discovering them trying to steal from the construction site. To calm Linda, Willy denies any wrongdoing on Biff's part; yet, Willy turns around and accepts Ben's praise of Biff as "nervy." Willy then boasts of his sales achievements after Charley has lamented the failure of his own New England salesman.

Ben exits after congratulating Willy on "being first-rate with

your boys." Ben delivers his last words "with a certain vicious audacity," saying, "When I walked into the jungle, I was seventeen. When I walked out I was twenty-one. And, by God, I was rich!" The flashback ends as Willy replies, "That's just the spirit I want to imbue them with! To walk into a jungle! I was right! I was right! I was right!" Willy is now alone, talking to no one, until Linda enters, in nightgown and robe.

### Analysis

At the outset of this segment of the play, we find that Willy exaggerates about his ability and popularity as a salesman. Although this revelation may give us cause to call Willy arrogant, Miller makes Willy seem less pompous and more sympathetic by having him confess to his own anxieties about being fat, foolish, and too talkative. At this moment, Willy reminds us of Bernard, who "is liked but not well liked," and Biff, who has not mastered a career. Thus, behind Willy's blustering anger and constant boasting lies an intense insecurity about whether he is liked and whether he is a failure as a businessman.

It is that insecurity, in all likelihood, that turns into confusion and rage after Willy remembers his affair with the woman in Boston. Consumed with self-hate and frustration after hearing how much his wife loves him, he is overwhelmed by the fact that Linda must mend her own stockings (when he gives new ones to the Boston woman) and by the stealing and cheating he did not discourage in Biff. Rather than confront his own dishonesty, however, Willy renews his deception by remaining silent about his affair and telling Linda, "There's nothing the matter with [Biff]! You want him to be a worm like Bernard? He's got spirit, personality...."

Charley is an example of someone who, in Willy's mind, does not have "spirit" or "personality," whereas Ben represents the epitome of successful "personality." Charley's general slowness and lack of skill with tools prompts Willy to think of him as unsuccessful, unimportant, and unmanly, but Willy does admit that Charley has people's respect in a way he does not. Furthermore, that respect has translated into business success for Charley, who can afford kindly to offer Willy a job. Willy's swollen pride will not allow him to accept the offer or to treat Charley civilly; instead, Willy

turns to his memory of Ben, someone who made a fortune on his adventuresome, charismatic personality rather than on simple hard work. We never learn exactly how Ben made his money, and Willy never asks, by which Miller implies Ben was either merely lucky or very ruthless in attaining his wealth. At one point, Ben engages in some friendly wrestling with Biff, but reminds the boy, "Never fight fair with a stranger, boy. You'll never get out of the jungle that way." Willy's view of the world reflects Ben's world in a way. Willy has convinced himself and his sons that life is a jungle from which only some people will emerge victorious; victory, according to this logic, results from cleverness, not necessarily from an honest work ethic.

Characters are said to be "lost" or "finding themselves" in the play up to this point, reflecting the fact that they have substituted cleverness and personality for knowing themselves. After his vision and flashback of Ben, Willy has shed the self-doubt that threatened to overcome him earlier in this section of the play. Miller has suggested that Willy experiences cycles of anxiety and confidence, with any realistic self-assessment usually succumbing to his belief in the rewards of personal attractiveness. However, the renewed energy and confidence seem to indicate that when reality begins to overwhelm Willy, he reverts to reverie, flashbacks, imaginary conversations, and megalomania. Although Willy must bear heavy responsibility for his ongoing predicament, the play also shows the way Willy has been misled by the myth of charm and cunning, represented here by Ben. Lacking any stable, self-determined identity, Willy has failed to defend himself against that myth.

### Study Questions

1. What do we learn about Willy's ability as a salesman as this section of the play begins?

2. Does Willy ever doubt that he is attractive and well liked?

3. What memory or daydream does Willy have immediately after he tells Linda, "You're the best there is"?

4. What gift does Willy not give to Linda, even though he does give it to someone else?

5. Why does Willy scream at Linda and Bernard to "Shut up!"?

6. Do Willy and Charley play cards in the present or in the past of a flashback?

7. Who is Ben and why does Willy admire him?

8. Why is the watchman chasing Biff?

9. What does Charley offer Willy as they play cards? Does Willy accept?

10. Does Willy's conversation with Ben convince Willy that he has been raising his sons correctly?

### Answers

1. We discover that Willy exaggerates; after telling Linda he did very well on his recent trip, he admits he is not a very successful salesman and becomes discouraged.

2. Yes. Despite trying to explain away his lack of success in sales, Willy does confess to Linda that he fears people think of him as fat, foolish, and too talkative.

3. Willy remembers or has a daydream about his affair with a woman in Boston.

4. He gives stockings to his mistress in Boston, but he does not give the same gift to Linda, who mends her own torn stockings.

5. After remembering the way he has betrayed his wife by having an affair, Willy becomes confused and frustrated when Linda and Bernard's questions remind him of Biff's questionable behavior. Willy yells "Shut up!" because the emotional pressure of the situation is overwhelming him.

6. They play cards in the present. After the extended flashback that began in Part 2, Willy finds himself still in the kitchen, where he went to make a sandwich. Hap comes downstairs to help his father to bed but leaves when Charley enters.

7. Ben is Willy's older brother, who is now dead but whom Willy remembers while playing cards with Charley. Willy admires

Ben because Ben represents the wealthy, heroic, charismatic ideal to which Willy urges his sons to aspire.

8.  The watchman is chasing Biff because he and Hap – at their father's request – have tried to steal material from a construction site.

9.  Charley, guessing that Willy is having trouble at work, offers him a job. Too proud to admit he is having difficulty, Willy does not accept and asks why Charley would insult him with such an offer.

10. Yes. When Ben tells Willy that he has been doing a "first-rate" job with his son, Willy is reassured that he has correctly prepared his sons to follow in Ben's footsteps.

### Suggested Essay Topics

1.  In this part of the play, we see several sides of Willy, some sympathetic and some rather unlikable. Write an essay that describes how it is possible for Willy to switch from anxious self-doubt at the beginning of the section to brash confidence at the end of it. Show how the starting and stopping of the flashbacks and imaginary conversations contribute to this change.

2.  Describe how Willy has taken Ben's life and his philosophy of the "jungle" as models for success. How has Willy shaped that philosophy to encompass life as a salesman?

# Act I, Part 4

### Summary

Part 4 covers the action up to the end of Act I.

The flashback involving Ben has ended, leaving Willy alone when Linda comes looking for him. In a dreamy state, still thinking of Ben, Willy has headed out of the house to take a short walk

despite the late hour. Woken up by Willy's loud, imagined conversation with Ben moments ago, Biff and Happy now come downstairs to talk with their mother about Willy. Surprised by the severity
of Willy's hallucinations, Biff asks why his mother had not told him
of Willy's condition. Linda responds that Willy's disturbed state
stems partly from Biff's failure to write Willy, to reconcile their differences, and to settle into a career.

When Biff implies that he is worried about Linda, she announces that she cannot care about her without expressing equal
concern for his father. Almost crying, she says, "I won't have anyone making [Willy] feel unwanted and low and blue....I know he's
not easy to get along with – nobody knows that better than me."
Biff protests that Willy has "never had an ounce of respect" for
Linda, but she insists on the need to treat Willy with kindness. "I
don't say he's a great man," Linda argues, "but he's a human being,
and a terrible thing is happening to him. So attention must be
paid."

She explains that Willy's company recently forced him to work
on commission, rather than for a salary, and that his old business
friends have died or retired, leaving him with few friendly customers. Linda makes a long speech revealing that Willy is too proud to
tell her that he now borrows $50 a week from Charley without tell-
ing her. After listening to his mother, Biff agrees to live at home
and help support the family. He refuses, however, to reconcile with
Willy, maintaining that the reason Willy originally threw him out
of the house was "Because I know he's a fake." Biff, though, declines to explain what he means by this comment.

Trying to impress upon Biff the seriousness of Willy's predicament, Linda discloses to Biff and Hap that their father has been
trying to kill himself. According to an insurance inspector, Willy's
several recent car accidents have been deliberate attempts to injure himself; furthermore, Linda believes Willy may kill himself with
gas from the heater using a hidden rubber pipe she recently discovered. The shock of this news scares Biff: "I've been remiss. I know
that, Mom. But now I'll stay, and I swear to you, I'll apply myself."

Just as Biff is again having doubts about his ability to adjust to
the business world, Willy returns from his walk and hears enough
of Biff's griping to become angry with him again. Biff and Willy

become frustrated with each other, but when Biff threatens to leave for good, Hap tells Willy that Biff plans to see Bill Oliver tomorrow. Seeing Willy's interest, Biff plays along and soon he and Hap have concocted the idea that Biff will ask Oliver for a loan to start a line of Loman brothers sporting goods, marketed through exhibition games that Biff and Hap will organize and play. The idea thrills Willy, who is convinced – in his characteristic salesman's optimism – that it "is a one-million-dollar idea" that will end Biff's problems. "I see great things for you kids," Willy tells Biff and Hap, "I think your troubles are over." Linda also begins to think the family's difficulties may turn around.

In his enthusiasm, Willy starts rattling off advice to Biff about how to act and what to wear when he asks Oliver for the loan. Willy warns Biff not to tell Oliver jokes or use a boyish word like "Gee," but also not to be too modest because "it's not what you say, it's how you say it – because personality always wins the day." Biff says little until Willy scolds Linda for interrupting his words of advice. Biff furiously tells his father to "stop yelling at her!" Apparently shamed, Willy's mood deflates, and he heads to his bedroom. Disappointed that Biff has made Willy unhappy again, Linda and Hap convince Biff to come upstairs and revive Willy's spirits before he falls asleep. Even before Biff enters Willy's bedroom, though, we see Willy already talking animatedly again about his confidence in Biff.

Willy's praise continues as Biff leaves the room. While Biff sits downstage smoking a cigarette, Willy and Linda reminisce with each other about Biff's glory days as a high school football player. As we hear their words, we see Biff remove the rubber pipe from behind the gas heater; holding it in his hand, he looks horrified and gazes up toward Willy's room, then heads up the stairs carrying the pipe.

### Analysis

In this section of the play, the audience sees how Linda has had to endure Willy's behavior and Biff's sullen anger at his father. Linda has been caught between Willy and Biff, trying to sympathize with both her husband and her son. Biff has not realized the way his resentment of Willy has caused Linda pain. Biff notices

oₙₗy Willy's shortcomings, Linda explains, and fails to remember how Willy has been a caring, protective, hard-working father.

Linda's several long speeches in this section reveal why she should not be described as a mindless, overly docile housewife. She manages the household finances; she deals with Willy's unpredictable moods; and she detects when Willy tries to conceal things from her (such as the money from Charley and the hidden rubber pipe). Furthermore, she acknowledges that "Willy is not easy to get along with." Within the Loman family, Linda is perhaps the most rational person. However, because of her gentle personality and because women of her day were not encouraged to be assertive, Linda rarely expresses any anger toward Willy or her sons. Her kind nature is momentarily interrupted when she scolds Biff and admits that getting along with Willy can be difficult; nevertheless, her temporary frustration actually signals her wish that the family can be happy and unified once again. Her tendency to hope for the best, in this sense, participates in Willy's unwillingness to face problems realistically. Although *Death of a Salesman* and Linda herself call so much attention to Willy's dignity as an ordinary "human being," we can also see Linda as someone very much like Willy – not a "great" person but still deserving of respect.

At this point in the play, it is difficult to know what to think about Biff's contention that Willy is a "fake." Although the audience may have considered Willy irritating at times, Biff refuses to say exactly why he calls Willy a fake and why Willy originally threw him out the house. Throughout this scene, Biff behaves somewhat childishly; his complaints about office jobs and about Willy are reasonable but also express a fair amount of selfishness and self-pity.

Willy's moods – like Biff's – change several times in this scene. Although Willy is hopeful again as he goes to bed, we must now question if the new possibility of Biff and Hap's business is enough to keep Willy from killing himself. Biff and Hap's business idea was created on the spur of the moment in order to please Willy, and so we must wonder what the consequences will be if Bill Oliver does not grant Biff the loan. That seems to be exactly what Biff wonders as he removes the rubber pipe from behind the heater: if I fail one more time, what will happen to my father? Willy and Linda's fond memory of Biff's glory days as a high school football player only place more pressure on Biff to live up to his long-faded success.

### Study Questions

1. Where does Linda lay the blame for Willy's disoriented, hallucinatory condition?

2. While trying to convince Biff that he should stop continually fighting with Willy, does Linda argue that Willy has no faults?

3. Why is it that "attention must be paid" to Willy?

4. Why must Willy borrow $50 every week from Charley?

5. According to Biff, why did Willy originally throw him out of the house many years ago?

6. What did Linda learn about Willy from the insurance inspector?

7. What hidden object has Linda recently discovered and why has it caused her to worry?

8. Why does Biff intend to ask Bill Oliver for a loan?

9. What does Willy think of Biff's idea to ask Oliver for a loan?

10. What does Biff remove from behind the gas heater?

### Answers

1. Linda believes that Willy's troubles stem partly from Biff's failure to write Willy, to reconcile their differences, and to settle into a career.

2. No. Linda admits Willy is "not easy to get along with – nobody knows that better than me."

3. Linda tells Biff and Hap that "attention must be paid" to Willy not because he is a great man, but simply because he is a human being – an aging man who is exhausted after working for so many years with very little to show for it.

4. He borrows the money because he is not earning very much as a salesman now that he is working on commission rather

than receiving a salary. His friendly customers have either died or retired, leaving Willy with few easy sales.

5.  Biff contends that Willy threw him out "because I know he's a fake," although Biff never explains precisely what he means by this.

6.  Linda learned that Willy's several recent car accidents were probably his deliberate attempts to injure himself – perhaps even attempts to commit suicide.

7.  Linda has discovered a rubber pipe that Willy has hidden. She is worried because she believes Willy may commit suicide by using the pipe to breath gas from the heater.

8.  Biff plans to ask Oliver for a loan so he and Hap can start a line of sporting goods.

9.  Willy is thrilled by the plan. He pesters Biff with advice about how to behave during the meeting with Oliver, but he calls the sporting goods line a "one-million-dollar idea."

10. He removes the rubber pipe that Linda said Willy might use to kill himself.

### Suggested Essay Topics

1.  In this section of the play we have learned a lot about Linda Loman. Write an essay that describes the way Linda sometimes shares Willy's wishful thinking but also exhibits independence and an awareness of Willy's shortcomings. Describe how Linda balances these different tendencies.

2.  Linda says that "attention must be paid" to Willy despite his faults. Write an essay in which you either support Linda's claim or argue against it. If Willy is a "fake," as Biff calls him, then does he deserve respect?

# SECTION THREE

# *Act II*

## Act II, Part 1

New Character:

**Howard Wagner:** *Willy's boss*

### *Summary*

Part I covers the action from the beginning of Act II until Howard Wagner says to Willy, "Pull yourself together, kid, there's people outside."

The act opens with bright, cheerful music as Linda sees Willy off to work. Both of them are in high spirits, feeling confident that Biff will receive the loan from Bill Oliver today. Linda tells Willy that Biff's "whole attitude seemed to be hopeful" when he left the house earlier in the morning. "He's heading for a change," replies Willy, who then remarks that he may buy some seeds tonight to plant a garden in the backyard.

Rather than starting on a sales trip today, Willy intends to go to his company's main office in the city and finally ask his boss, Howard, for a new, non-traveling job. Knowing that Biff's luck might improve has given Willy new determination, too. However, Willy's mood sours again when Linda reminds him to ask Howard for an advance in pay; several bills must be paid – the insurance premium, the car repair, the refrigerator, and the house payment. After this

house payment, though, Willy and Linda will own their house outright, ending 25 years of payments. Willy is heartened by that thought and Linda's news that he must meet Biff and Hap for dinner in the city: "Biff came to me this morning, Willy, and he said, 'Tell Dad, we want to blow him to a big meal.' Be there six o'clock. You and your boys are going to have dinner." The expectation is that at the dinner Biff will announce that he received the loan and that Willy will announce that he has a better job. As Willy leaves the house, he sees a pair of Linda's stockings and demands that she stop mending them because "it gets me nervous." After Willy has left, Linda receives a telephone call from Biff, who wants to make sure Linda told Willy about dinner. Before the conversation ends, Linda reminds Biff to "be sweet to [Willy] tonight, dear. Be loving to him. Because he's only a little boat looking for a harbor."

The scene then switches to Howard Wagner's office, where Willy is trying to ask for a new job. Howard, many years younger than Willy, is busy playing with a "wire recorder" – in other words, a tape recorder, which was a relatively new invention at that time. Howard enthusiastically plays recordings of his daughter whistling, his son reciting state capitals, and his wife shyly wondering what to say to the machine. Howard encourages Willy to buy a recorder, suggesting that it can be used to record radio programs. "Supposing you wanna hear Jack Benny['s radio program], see?" he says. "But you can't be home at that hour. So you tell the maid to turn the radio on when Jack Benny comes on, and [the recorder] automatically goes on with the radio."

Eventually, Willy manages to tell Howard that he's tired and would prefer not to travel anymore. Howard answers that there are no openings to be a salesman in the store. "[W]here am I going to put you, kid?" he asks Willy. When Howard states "you gotta admit, business is business," Willy launches into a long story about how he began as a traveling salesman very young in life. His inspiration, Willy says, came from watching the way an older salesman, Dave Singleman, could at age 84 make sales with a simple phone call. When Singleman died, hundreds of buyers and salesmen came to his funeral. Such friendship and gratitude, though, is not possible now, says Willy, because all the "personality" has been taken out of the business.

Howard does not change his mind. Willy becomes insistent and reminds Howard that Willy has worked for the company since before Howard was born, back when Howard's father owned the company. Howard still does not budge, and when he leaves the room Willy realizes that he has been yelling at Howard. When Howard returns, Willy feels ashamed; Willy states he will go to Boston and continue to be a traveling salesman. Rather than accept Willy's offer, Howard fires him, telling him "I think you need a good long rest, Willy."

Willy is stunned. When he tells Howard that he *must* earn money, Howard suggests that Willy's sons support him. Willy admits that Biff and Hap are "working on a very big deal," but adds "I can't throw myself on my sons. I'm not a cripple!" Howard does not give in. Asking Willy to return the company's sample cases, Howard leaves the office as he says to Willy, "Pull yourself together, kid, there's people outside."

### Analysis

With the new day, Linda and Willy have renewed hopes. By this point in the play, though, the audience might wonder if – considering the many past disappointments of the Lomans – they should be more cautious. When Willy announces that he will try to plant a garden in the yard, Miller means that once again Willy will try to plant seeds of hope and change. Linda reminds Willy, though, that "not enough sun gets back there. Nothing'll grow anymore"; with these lines, Miller seems to say that Willy's hope is misplaced and futile – his wish for a better life stands little chance of coming true. The wish has little chance not only because Willy might be a "fake," but because the world has little sympathy for an ordinary person like Willy. Although the American dream invites people to believe that a better life is within their grasp, even Willy's decades of hard work may not be enough to ensure a stable living.

Willy and Linda's bills remind us that they are struggling to make ends meet. While the end of house payments is a bright spot, bills will keep coming. And when Willy sees Linda's stockings, he is reminded that not only has he had trouble making money to buy Linda new stockings, but he has cheated on her by having an affair with another woman.

Willy's behavior in Howard's office should remind the audience of how Willy told Biff *not* to behave when visiting Bill Oliver. Willy counseled Biff not to be timid, but Willy *is* timid, asking Howard for $65 a week then $50 and finally $40; and when Howard looks for a cigarette lighter, Willy hands it to him, even though Willy had told Biff not to do small, demeaning things like pick up a fallen package when trying to assert oneself with a boss. Throughout this scene, Howard calls Willy "kid," even though Howard is only Biff's age. Calling Willy "kid" shows Howard's lack of respect for Willy.

Howard signifies the success and privilege that neither Willy nor his own son Biff has had. Howard suggests that Willy buy a wire recorder, but Willy could never afford the $150 it costs. Similarly, unlike Howard, Willy does not have a maid who could turn on the recorder in the middle of the day. Instead, Willy has a wife, Linda, who must do all of the household chores herself. Thus, Howard's family reminds us of the happiness and prosperity Willy once hoped would be his own. Moreover, Howard contrasts starkly with Biff, who has neither a family nor a job at this advanced stage in his life.

When he recounts his admiration for Dave Singleman, Willy describes someone who mastered the "personality" of selling. Willy has not had the same success, partially because his old buyers have retired and partially because Willy's personality may not be extremely likable. The image of Dave Singleman's well-attended funeral is important because it differs so much from the image of a sad Willy contemplating a solitary suicide rather than life.

As Willy is fired, we see him become increasingly desperate. He really does seem like "a little boat looking for a harbor," as Linda described him. By firing Willy, Howard implies that not only is Willy a bad salesman but also that his personality is an embarrassment to the company. Throughout his life, Willy felt sure that his personality would bring him business success, but it has not. Willy's failure can be blamed on his own annoying behavior and arrogance (remember his mean attitude toward Bernard and Charley, as well as how he cheated on his wife and how he permitted Biff to cheat at school). However, Willy should not bear all the blame for his failure, the play seems to say. Despite Willy's faults, he has endured many years on the road as a salesman and has made barely enough money to get by. Howard's excuse that "business is business" sounds awfully cold-hearted, since it equates Willy's value as a human being with his ability to make money for the company. The play indirectly proposes that Willy's failure cannot be blamed entirely on him as an individual. American culture – especially the way it equates money with a person's value – is also responsible for Willy's lack of enduring beliefs and for abandoning him in his time of need. Somehow the competitive "laws of business" fail to ensure the humane treatment of all citizens.

### Study Questions

1. In the morning, Willy tells Linda he will buy something for the backyard. What does he intend to buy and what does Miller seem to mean by this purchase?

2. As he leaves the house, what does Willy plan to ask Howard?

3. What message does Linda relay to Willy from Biff and Hap?

4. Why do Linda's stockings make Willy nervous?

5. What machine does Howard show Willy? How might Howard's comments about this machine make Willy uncomfortable?

6. Does Willy receive a non-traveling job or does he continue in his old job as traveling salesman?

7. Who is Dave Singleman and what significance does he hold for Willy?

8. What reasons does Howard give for not granting Willy's requests and finally firing him?

9. Why does Willy mention Howard's father?

10. Where does Howard suggest Willy look for support?

### Answers

1. Willy intends to buy some seeds to plant a garden in the backyard. The seeds seem to signify Willy's renewed hope, but because of his lack of success in the past we must question whether anything will change for Willy.

2.  Willy plans to ask Howard for a non-traveling sales job. In addition, he plans to ask for an advance in pay so he can settle his bills.

3.  Linda tells Willy that he should meet Biff and Hap at a restaurant at six o'clock because his sons want to buy him dinner and celebrate; at this point, however, Biff has not even visited Oliver, so the celebration is not ensured.

4.  Although Willy never explains, we can guess that seeing Linda mend stockings reminds him of his inability to buy her new stockings and of his betrayal of her with another woman, to whom he did give stockings.

5.  The machine is a wire recorder, similar to today's tape recorder. As Howard shows the recorder to Willy, he mentions his happy family, which may make Willy feel uncomfortable because his family has not been happy lately. Furthermore, Willy does not make enough money to hire a maid or buy a recorder.

6.  Neither. Howard refuses to give Willy a non-traveling job and moments later fires Willy, meaning Willy loses his job as traveling salesman, too.

7.  Singleman was a salesman whom Willy admired for having been so successful and well liked that at age 84 he could make sales by phone. Hundreds of people came to Singleman's funeral to express their friendship, a measure of respect that Willy has aspired to achieve.

8.  When Willy asks for a non-traveling job, Howard answers that there are no openings now, saying "business is business." When Willy offers to remain in his traveling job, Howard fires him, telling Willy to take "a good long rest." By firing Willy, Howard implies that not only is Willy not a good salesman but his personality is an embarrassment to the company.

9.  Willy mentions Howard's father in an attempt to make Howard realize that he deserves respect. Willy has worked for the company since before Howard's birth, back when

Howard's father owned it. Those long years of loyal service, Willy contends, should be rewarded.

10. Howard suggests Willy's sons could help support him financially, but Willy does not respond well to the idea.

### Suggested Essay Topics

1. Write an essay in which you describe how Willy's love of "personality" conforms to Howard's idea that "business is business." As you describe the fact that both attitudes are based on competition, also point out how Willy's concept of business is, in the end, not exactly the same as Howard's.

2. Write an essay that discusses the way Miller seems to pair characters or to see one character in another. For example, describe how Willy reminds us of Biff when asking for a new job; how Howard is a successful version of Willy and Biff; or how Dave Singleman represents Willy's unachieved view of himself.

# Act II, Part 2

### Summary

Part 2 covers the action up to when Willy says "Put up your hands!" to Charley.

The previous section ends with Howard leaving his office. Willy remains and the lights change. Ben's music begins to play, and Willy begins talking to him as he enters from the right carrying a suitcase and an umbrella. Ben tells Willy he has finished his business trip to Alaska and must soon board a boat to return to Africa. From this information the audience realizes that after getting fired Willy has begun daydreaming again and that a flashback has begun. Even though Ben is in a rush, Willy needs to talk to him: "Ben, nothing's working out. I don't know what to do." Ben offers Willy a job supervising his lumber operations in Alaska; encouraging Willy's desire

to do manly, outdoor work, Ben says, "Screw on your fists and you can fight for a fortune up there."

Linda joins Willy and Ben, but she does not approve of moving the family to Alaska. Frightened of Ben and angry with him, Linda insists that Willy is doing well enough already: "Enough to be happy right here, right now." Then she asks Willy "Why must everybody conquer the world?" To convince Willy not to go, Linda reminds Willy that old man Wagner said Willy could one day become a member of the firm, causing Willy to think Alaska may not be necessary: "I am building something with this firm, Ben, and if a man is building something he must be on the right track, mustn't he?" Willy gains additional confidence when Linda reminds him of Dave Singleman's success.

Biff and Hap (as teenagers) enter. Biff is in his football sweater and Hap carries the rest of Biff's uniform. "Three great universities are begging" for Biff, Willy tells Ben, "and from there the sky's the limit, because it's not what you do, Ben. It's who you know and the smile on your face." As Willy continues to claim that in this country a person's fortune can be built on the basis of being liked, Ben begins to leave. When Willy asks once more, "Ben, am I right?", Ben responds only by repeating that Alaska could make Willy "rich!"

After Ben has gone, Willy and the rest of the family get ready to leave for Biff's big football game. Bernard arrives and pleads to carry some of Biff's equipment so he, like Hap, can accompany Biff into the clubhouse at Ebbets Field, the famous baseball stadium where the All-Scholastic Championship of New York football game will be played. Charley enters just as everyone is about to leave. Pretending not to know it is the day of Biff's important game, Charley asks Willy if he wants to play cards. Charley continues to joke with Willy, telling Biff to hit a home run at Ebbets Field, but Willy becomes very angry. Willy tells Charley he won't be laughing after Biff becomes as famous and wealthy as Red Grange. Charley continues to tease Willy, pretending not to recognize Red Grange (an extremely well-known football player at that time). Willy becomes so frustrated that he challenges Charley to a fight: "Who the hell do you think you are, better than everybody else? You don't know everything, you big, ignorant, stupid.... Put up your hands!" Charley walks away as Willy follows him.

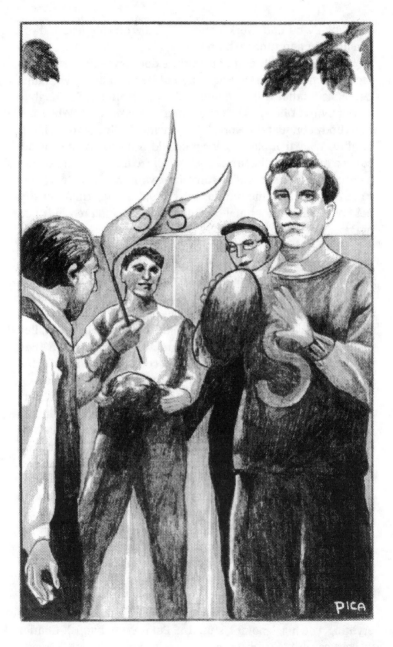

### Analysis

This section of the play can be read as Willy's daydream or memory. After being fired, he thinks back to this moment many years ago when he chose a life as a salesman rather a new life of adventure and possibility in Alaska. Because he has not enjoyed Dave Singleman's success and popularity, he must now concede that his many years of work did not really "build" him anything. The fact that Biff has not become a famous football player also adds to his regret: Willy did not prove Charley wrong.

Willy sees himself teaching his sons the same masculine sense of adventure and self-reliance that he admires in Ben. Finally, though, Ben's sense of superiority may differ from Willy's own arrogance and belief in "personality." Whereas Willy often tries to use a smile as a shortcut, Ben appears to have made his fortune without depending on the approval and favors of others. Ben appears selfish, but he is also "self-made" in a way Willy is not.

When Linda argues against Alaska, we notice how she is repeating what Willy has told her. We begin to doubt if old man Wagner ever really promised Willy a promotion. Likewise, we become suspicious of the Dave Singleman story: was he really so popular? What makes Willy believe such success is possible? At the very least, we recognize that Willy has always childishly based his life's hopes on only a few promises and stories. In order to continue in his job and present social position, Willy needs to believe that he may one day be successful and widely liked. When he cannot laugh at Charley's teasing, however, we see the way Willy's need to believe in himself has made him into an angry, resentful person. He has based his self-esteem heavily on his wealth, his popularity, and Biff's success as a football player. Linda's contention that Willy should "be happy right here" shows how she distrusts the impulse to always "conquer"; however, it is hard to believe that Willy will ever be happy as long as he expects successful results from cheating, smiling, and a rude "personality."

### Study Questions

1. Who does Willy "meet" after Howard fires him?

2. When Willy tells his brother that "nothing is working out," what opportunity does Ben offer Willy?

3. What does Linda think of Ben's offer?

4. What two things does Linda mention to persuade Willy of her opinion about his current job?

5. Does Willy accept Ben's offer?

6. When Willy asks one last time if Ben approves of his ideas about business and the way he has raised his son, how does Ben respond?

7. Why is it an important day for Biff?

8. Does Charley expect Willy to accept his invitation to play cards?

9. Why does Willy challenge Charley to fight?

10. What comment does this scene as a whole make about Willy's mood after being fired by Howard?

### Answers

1. Willy "meets" Ben, his older brother. More precisely, Willy remembers or daydreams the meeting, which appears to the audience as a flashback to time several years ago when Ben visited Willy after a trip to Alaska.

2. Ben offers Willy the chance to work for him in Alaska.

3. Linda does not want Willy to accept the job in Alaska. She thinks Willy should be happy enough in his present job.

4. To persuade Willy not to accept the job in Alaska, Linda reminds Willy that old man Wagner has said Willy may become a member in the firm; she also reminds him of Dave Singleman's success as a salesman.

5. No. Willy decides not to accept the job in Alaska and to remain in his sales job.

6. Ben neither outright approves or disapproves. However, Ben's remark that Alaska could make Willy "rich!" means that Ben probably does not entirely endorse Willy's decisions; Ben seems to say that Willy would be better off going to Alaska.

7. It is an important day because Biff will play in the All-Scho-

lastic Championship of New York – an important high school football game at Ebbets Field.

8.  No. Charley asks Willy to play cards as a way of teasing him. Charley only pretends not to know that Willy and Biff and the rest of the family are leaving for the football game.

9.  Willy becomes angry with Charley for joking about Biff's big football game.

10. This section – Willy's daydream or memory – represents a happier moment in Willy's life, a moment when he had more faith in his sales career and in Biff's future success. After being fired, though, this memory cannot bring Willy much happiness, since it must remind him of when he refused the possible wealth of Alaska and continued to believe blindly that both he and Biff would become successful on the basis of merely being liked. In addition, as a whole, this section shows Willy's tendency to escape reality through daydreams of real or imaginary conversations.

### Suggested Essay Topics

1.  Contrast Willy with Ben. Willy seems to think that he leads a life somehow like Ben's. Besides the fact that Ben is rich and Willy is not, what separates them? You might begin by comparing Ben's willingness to travel to remote places such as Alaska and Africa with Willy's reluctance to disrupt his own rather ordinary life.

2.  Should Willy be "happy right here, right now," as Linda says? Willy has a wife and two sons who love him, so why should he be unhappy? Examine how Willy continually *plans* for his own success and happiness but always seems unsatisfied, even angry. You might start by suggesting that Willy cannot meet the requirements for success that he sets for himself. Willy says "the sky's the limit" when "it's who you know and the smile on your face," but who does Willy know and what has his smile earned him?

# Act II, Part 3

New Character:

**Jenny:** *Charley's secretary*

### *Summary*

Part 3 covers the action up to when Willy says, "Charley, you're the only friend I got. Isn't that a remarkable thing?"

The flashback in which Willy challenges Charley to fight has ended, but Willy is still heard talking loudly offstage. The lights come up on a new scene: Bernard, now an adult, and Jenny, Charley's secretary, in Charley's office. After being fired, Willy has come to Charley's office – as he does every week, Jenny tells Bernard. Jenny has work to do and asks Bernard to deal with Willy, who is obviously very disoriented, talking to himself as if he were in the flashback of Part 2. As Willy enters, he seems to flirt with Jenny; however, pathos fills the moment when Jenny asks, "How've you been feeling?" and Willy responds, "Not much any more," indicating his emotional numbness. Willy then becomes polite and formal when he notices Bernard. As an adult, Bernard now strikes a very impressive figure; he still wears glasses but is mature and self-assured.

Willy is surprised to see Bernard, who is now a lawyer and on his way to Washington, DC, where he will argue a case. Explaining why he has two tennis rackets with him, Bernard states that while in Washington he will play tennis with a friend who has his own tennis court. Impressed with the kind of friends Bernard keeps, Willy boasts that Bill Oliver called Biff back East for a very important deal. However, Willy cannot maintain this deception for long and soon asks Bernard, "Why didn't [Biff] ever catch on? .... His life ended after that Ebbets Field game. From the age of seventeen nothing good ever happened to him."

In an attempt to figure out Biff's lack of motivation and success, Bernard asks Willy if years ago he told Biff not to go to summer school to make up the math class he flunked. Had Biff gone to summer school he would have graduated from high school. Willy responds angrily: "Me? I begged him to go. I ordered him to go!"

Willy becomes increasingly defensive as Bernard explains that he remembers Biff planning to go to summer school but then changing his mind after a trip to Boston to see Willy. Upon returning from the trip, Bernard says, Biff burned his own sneakers, the ones on which he had written "University of Virginia," which was the college Biff had wanted to attend. Biff fought and cried with Bernard for some unexplained reason, which is why Bernard now wants to know "What happened in Boston, Willy?"

Willy denies anything happened and soon Charley walks in and the conversation changes. As Bernard leaves for Washington, Charley says proudly to Willy, "How do like this kid? Gonna argue a case in front of the Supreme Court." Bernard exits, but Willy is left in awe of Bernard, wondering why Bernard did not mention such important news. Charley replies that Bernard does not have to mention it – "he's gonna do it." Trying to return to work, Charley gives Willy $50, but Willy asks him for $110 since he has an insurance payment due.

Charley offers Willy a job working for him at $50 a week, but Willy insists that he already has a job. Charley then asks Willy why his job does not seem to earn him any money. Willy admits Howard fired him today but still cannot understand it; Willy always believed that success would come "if a man was impressive, and well liked." Charley tries to tell him that business success depends not on being well liked, but on having something to sell, a fact Willy as a salesman should have learned. When Willy refuses again to accept the job, Charley calls him jealous but gives him the insurance money anyway. Willy becomes subdued, thinking aloud that after so many years of work "you end up worth more dead than alive." Charley responds forcefully, "Willy, nobody's worth nothin' dead."

### *Analysis*

Meeting the adult Bernard, we see that the meek bookworm whom Willy once called "anemic" has grown up to be more successful and likable than Biff and Hap. Bernard's affluence and elevated social status reveal themselves in his occupation as a lawyer arguing a case in front of the Supreme Court and in his friend who owns a tennis court. Furthermore, tennis itself – unlike football, which Biff played – seems like a sport for successful, upper-class, sophisticated people.

Throughout this entire section of the play, Willy alternates between asking openly for help, explanations, and advice, *and* nervously lying (about having a job, about Biff's success). When Bernard questions Willy about what happened in Boston, we begin to feel that Willy knows something that he will not admit, perhaps not even to himself. Up to this point in the play, we have been inclined to think that Biff's problems and his distrust of Willy do not stem from one particular event; however, we must now wonder exactly what did take place in Boston, those many years ago when Biff visited Willy after flunking math. We may remember that Boston was where Willy had his affair with The Woman, but at this stage in the play we can only wonder if that affair has any connection to why Biff never went to summer school and also to why Biff gets angriest at his father when he is defending his mother from Willy's cruelties and verbal abuse.

Charley's remark – that Bernard does not have to mention something because "he's going to do it" – reminds us that Willy has always been all talk and no action. Seeing Bernard and Charley's success alongside Willy and Biff's lack of success, we realize the way Willy's desire to be "well liked" has failed him. Furthermore, not even Charley truly likes Willy, since Willy has long looked down on him and even now acts too proud to accept a job from him. Rather than admit the error of over-emphasizing the importance of "personality," Willy initially lies about his job and about Biff. Willy feels ashamed but has never been able to stop hoping that events would turn around.

However, when Willy says "you end up worth more dead than alive," we sense his despair rather than the usual optimism. Death, Willy implies, might be equal to or better than facing failure honestly. If we consider Willy's words less metaphorically, we wonder whether he means that, if he dies, the insurance policy will pay his family more money than he could earn for them while still alive. At this moment, Willy appears to contemplate suicide as a way of solving his problems. Charley seems to detect the seriousness of Willy's despair. By saying "nobody's worth nothin' dead," Charley implies that death solves nothing; through Charley's line, Miller may also be reminding us that Willy's family would not receive life insurance money if Willy's death were found to be a suicide. As the scene ends, the audience might also detect the way Willy equates friendship with the loaning of money when he tells Charley, "You're the only friend I got."

### Study Questions

1. How has Bernard changed from when he was a boy?

2. What is Bernard's job and what will he do in Washington, DC?

3. Why did Biff not graduate from high school?

4. What big question does Bernard ask Willy? How does Willy respond?

5. According to Charley, why doesn't Bernard mention the reason for his trip to Washington, DC?

6. Why does Willy ask Charley to borrow more than the usual $50?

7. Other than a loan of money, what does Charley offer Willy? Does Willy accept?

8. Does Willy conceal from Charley the fact that Howard fired him?

9. What does Charley say about Willy's belief that success would come "if a man was impressive, and well liked"?

10. What might Willy mean when he says, "you end up worth more dead than alive"?

### Answers

1. As an adult, Bernard is mature, likable, self-assured, and athletic – very different from the meek, timid, overly studious teenager whom Willy called "anemic."

2. Bernard is a lawyer and will argue a case in front of the Supreme Court in Washington, DC.

3. Biff did not graduate because he flunked a math class. Al-

though he planned to attend summer school to make up the class, he never went. The reasons he decided not to attend remain unclear.

4. Bernard asks, "What happened in Boston, Willy?" In other words, did Biff's visit to see Willy in Boston have anything to do with Biff's decision not to attend summer school? Willy replies that nothing happened in Boston, but this quick, defensive response makes us wonder if he is hiding something.

5. Charley explains that Bernard does not have to mention he will argue a case in front of the Supreme Court – "he's gonna do it." Unlike Bernard, Willy has always been all talk and no action.

6. Willy asks to borrow $110, rather than $50, because his insurance payment is due.

7. Charley, as he has done before, offers Willy a job working for him. Charley becomes insulted when Willy will not accept the job but will borrow money. Willy never explains to Charley why he will not accept the job.

8. At first, Willy does conceal the fact that Howard fired him. He pretends to have a job. However, he finally does admit to Charley that he has been fired.

9. Charley tries to tell Willy that business success depends not on being well liked, but on having something to sell, a fact Willy as a salesman should have learned.

10. Willy may mean that, if he dies, the insurance policy will pay his family more money than he could earn for them while still alive. His words also imply that he may be thinking about killing himself, although he does not seem to acknowledge that the insurance money would not be paid if it can be shown he committed suicide.

### Suggested Essay Topics

1. Write an essay in which you use this section of the play to compare Bernard with Biff. Show how Bernard has become

exactly the kind of successful and likable person that Willy wanted Biff to be.

2.   Use Charley's remark – about how it is unnecessary to boast about something if you're going to *do* it – to write an essay that examines the way Willy continually *says* what he will do but never actually *does* it. Look again at Willy's conversations with Bernard and Charley in this section and try to decide whether Willy lies when he boasts or if he actually believes what he says, or both.

# Act II, Part 4

New Characters:

**Stanley:** *a young waiter at the restaurant where Biff, Happy, and Willy meet*

**Miss Forsythe:** *a woman whom Biff and Happy meet in the restaurant. (In the text she is referred to as simply "Girl" before her name is given.)*

**Letta:** *Miss Forsythe's friend, who eventually joins her, Biff, and Happy at the restaurant*

***Summary***

Part 4 covers the action up to when Stanley calls to Hap, "Mr. Loman! Mr. Loman!"

The scene has changed to a restaurant. Hap finds a table with the help of Stanley, a waiter who knows Hap and treats him very well. Bending the truth, Hap tells Stanley that Biff is an important cattle man out West; Hap orders champagne, announcing that Biff and Willy will soon arrive to celebrate the brothers' new business. Before Stanley exits, Hap asks him also to bring some champagne to a very beautiful woman at a nearby table. Introducing himself to the woman, Miss Forsythe, Hap pretends to work for a champagne company. When Biff arrives moments later, Hap continues

lying: he pretends that he attend West Point (the prestigious army college) and that Biff is actually the quarterback for the New York Giants professional football team.

Hap asks Miss Forsythe to sit with them and to find a friend for Biff. Hap sees that Biff is uninterested in the beautiful Miss Forsythe and asks, "Where's the old confidence, Biff?" When she leaves to make a phone call, Biff explains that he did not receive the loan from Bill Oliver. In fact, Oliver did not even recognize Biff. Furthermore, Biff himself finally remembered that he had not really been a salesman for Oliver. As a result, Biff confesses, "… I realized what a ridiculous lie my whole life has been! We've been talking in a dream for fifteen years. I was a shipping clerk." When Oliver and his secretary momentarily left Biff alone, he stole an expensive fountain pen and then ran out of the building. Now in agony over his self-deception and lack of self-restraint, Biff wants Hap to help him speak to Willy. Willy has thought Biff fails so often simply to spite or anger Willy, but Biff just wants Willy to "understand that I'm not the man somebody lends that kind of money to." Hap urges Biff to postpone telling Willy any bad news because "Dad is never so happy as when he's looking forward to something."

When Willy arrives, Biff (who is already slightly drunk) tells him, "Let's hold on to the facts tonight, Pop. We're not going to get anywhere bullin' around. I was a shipping clerk for Oliver, not a salesman." Willy treats this news as a minor detail, declaring, "I'm not interested in stories about the past or any crap of that kind because the woods are burning, boys, you understand? There's a big blaze going on all around. I was fired today." Willy, however, does not want to discuss losing his job; instead, he wants to hear some good news from Biff so he will have something positive to tell Linda tonight. After hearing this, Biff has even greater trouble trying to tell Willy about the loan. Willy keeps interrupting Biff, commanding he spit out the good news, and Hap pretends that Biff's meeting with Oliver was in fact a success. As Biff's anxiety continues to increase, Willy begins to think that either Biff never went to the office or Biff insulted Oliver.

While Biff struggles to finish speaking, Willy's thoughts come alive: in the background we see a flashback scene in which the young Bernard rushes to inform Linda that Biff has flunked math and will not graduate high school. Remembering or hallucinating this scene, Willy suddenly yells, "If you hadn't flunked you'd've been set by now!" Biff and Hap cannot hear or see the flashback, but the audience learns that after flunking, Biff has gone to Boston to see Willy. Although Biff and Hap have no idea why Willy has begun yelling in the restaurant, Biff keeps explaining and finally finishes recounting the truth about his meeting with Oliver. Willy comes out of his daze momentarily to notice the stolen pen, but another flashback begins as we hear a hotel phone operator tell someone that Mr. Loman is not in his room. Willy's frantic, scared anger seems directed at the operator's voice now, but Biff and Hap become so confused and frightened at Willy's crazy behavior that they change the story about Oliver.

Eventually they convince Willy that Oliver is actually still considering the business proposal and will have lunch with Biff tomorrow, at which time Biff will have another chance to "make an impression." Once Willy becomes clearheaded again, however, Biff tries to say he cannot attend the meeting or return the stolen pen. If he does attend, Biff explains, Oliver will remember that Biff stole the basketballs years ago and thus will know that taking the pen was not an accident this time. Willy grows mad and hits Biff, convinced Biff is spiting him by refusing to attend the lunch meeting. "I'm no good, can't you see what I am?" Biff responds, in a desperate attempt to show he is not acting out of spite.

As Miss Forsythe returns with her friend, Letta, Willy begins to hear the laughing voice of the Boston woman and excuses himself to go to the washroom. While he is away, Hap asks the two women where they should all go tonight; angry that Hap would leave Willy behind, Biff accuses Hap of not caring for their father and shows Hap the rubber pipe he took from behind the heater. Biff exits, almost crying, but Hap and the women follow him, planning to persuade him to join them for a fun night on the town. Leaving the restaurant, Hap tells the two women that Willy is not really his father: "He's just a guy." Shouting for Stanley and the check, Hap and the women leave the stage. When Stanley calls indignantly, "Mr. Loman! Mr. Loman!" we begin to suspect that Hap's shouting may conceal his intention of not paying the check, possibly a frequent habit for him.

### *Analysis*

This scene begins by exposing Hap's tendencies to lie to impress people, especially a woman to whom he is sexually attracted. His untruths – about attending West Point, about working for a champagne company, about Biff being a cattle man, and then about Biff playing for the Giants – may seem relatively harmless. However, when he helps Biff lie to Willy about the meeting with Oliver, we perceive how his lies also keep other people from facing reality. Finally, when Hap denies Willy is his father, he does so in part to impress Miss Forsythe. That denial fits Hap's pattern, as Miller described it earlier, of "never allowing himself to turn his face toward defeat," especially in a circumstance in which a woman might reject him if he told the truth. The possibility that he may be trying to avoid paying the check signals one more instance of Hap's comfort with cheating and betrayal.

Biff tries very hard to stop lying. After going to Oliver's office and stealing the pen, Biff finally understands how his life has been a "ridiculous lie." He realizes that he had begun believing the exaggerations and falsehoods that he, Willy, and Hap have always been so quick to make up. However, when confessing to dishonesty might mean pushing his father toward suicide, then Biff feels split and agonized. Hap, like Willy, can see no other alternative but continuing to deceive oneself and others (Linda, for example). Determined to remain "happy," though he too may be suffering, Hap attempts to avoid both the agony Biff undergoes and the loss of control Willy experiences.

Willy feels despondent after being fired, remembering Ben's Alaska offer, and visiting Charley. The principles and certainties by which he lived for so long have vanished in a "big blaze going all around." Consequently, he asks for some good news for Linda, which suggests that Linda constitutes Willy's last safe sense of himself; if she gives up hope, then he will never recover. Yet there is certainly irony in the fact that Willy asks for good news for Linda when Willy himself so desperately needs good news. And, while good news, to Willy, always means money, who knows how much happier Linda would have been if "good news" were that her husband has not been unfaithful to her? As Biff recounts bad news, Willy slips further into daydream and hallucination. Eventually, prompted by the Boston woman's voice, he leaves the table seeking the door of the hotel room, then catches himself and says he is going to the bathroom. Because the return of Miss Forsythe and Letta interrupts Willy's argument with Biff, we do not know if Willy believed that Biff really could meet Oliver for lunch. Clearly, though, Willy is unable or unwilling to face facts or forgive Biff, as Biff hoped he would. Hap's decision to leave the restaurant and avoid Willy is heartless, but we must remember that Biff has also left rather than deal with Willy. Neither brother wants to confront Willy; doing so would mean confronting themselves and their own failures, as well as increasing their father's own emotional turmoil.

### Study Questions

1. What lies does Hap tell and why?

2. Did Bill Oliver give Biff the loan? Does Biff tell Hap that he got the loan or not?

3. What particular memory causes Biff to exclaim, "I realized what a ridiculous lie my whole life has been"?

4. What did Biff steal from Oliver's office? Why?

5. What does Willy want to tell Linda?

6. What are the three flashbacks, memories, or hallucinations that Willy experiences while talking to Biff and Hap?

7. What story do Biff and Hap concoct when Willy's behavior becomes increasingly confusing and frightening?

8. Why does Biff tell Willy, "I'm no good, can't you see what I am?"

9. Why does Willy excuse himself from the table to go to the bathroom?

10. Do Biff, Hap, and Willy leave the restaurant together?

### Answers

1. He lies to Stanley by telling him that Biff is a big cattle man. He lies to Miss Forsythe by telling her that he sells champagne, that he went to West Point, and that Biff is the Gi-

ants' quarterback. These lies are designed to impress Stanley and especially Miss Forsythe, whom Hap sexually desires.

2. Biff tells Hap the truth: Bill Oliver did not give Biff the loan.

3. Biff remembers that he was only a shipping clerk for Bill Oliver and never a salesman. Convincing himself he was a salesman strikes Biff as an example of how he has been living in a dream.

4. Biff stole an expensive fountain pen. However, he can think of no explanation for having taken it. He may have been motivated by a desire to possess some of Oliver's wealth, a desire to spite Oliver for not remembering him, or a desire purposely to hurt his chances for the kind of responsible career from which he has always retreated.

5. A little good news. After having lost his job, Willy wants to have something positive to tell Linda when he returns home. He hopes the good news will be that Oliver has given Biff the loan.

6. First, Willy sees a flashback in which Bernard tells Linda that Biff has flunked math. Second, Willy hears a hotel phone operator tell someone that Mr. Loman is not in his room. Third, Willy hears the laughing voice of the Boston woman. The audience experiences all three along with Willy, but Biff and Hap do not.

7. They tell Willy that Bill Oliver is still considering Biff's proposal and that Biff has a chance to convince Oliver at a lunch meeting tomorrow.

8. Biff wants desperately to end the conflict between him and his father by making sure Willy knows that Biff did not intentionally offend Oliver out of spite for Willy.

9. Willy says he is going to the bathroom after catching himself in a hallucination in which, prompted by the Boston woman's voice, he wants to open the door of the hotel room.

10. No. While Willy is away from the table, Biff leaves after arguing with Hap. Hap soon follows, saying to Miss Forsythe and Letta that Willy is not really his father.

***Suggested Essay Topics***

1.  Use this section of the play to write an essay that explores the way Miller begins and ends flashbacks, memories, or hallucinations. For instance, show how Willy's anger with Biff's failure to get the loan triggers his vision of Bernard telling Linda about Biff flunking math in high school. In addition, discuss the way Miller overlaps Willy's hallucinatory lines with Biff and Hap's regular conversation.

2.  During much of the play, Biff and Hap seem very similar in the way they have both adopted Willy's capacity for self-deception. However, the brothers are also different from each other. Use this section of the play to write an essay that contrasts Happy and Biff. You might begin by showing how Hap never really feels guilty about his own behavior in the way that Biff feels about his.

# Act II, Part 5

***Summary***

Part 5 covers the action up to when Linda says, "He's planting the garden!"

After Biff, Hap, and the two women leave the restaurant, Willy's daydream involving the Boston woman becomes a full-fledged flashback. The Woman is in a black slip and Willy is buttoning his shirt. We hear raw, sexy music as The Woman teases Willy, telling him to stop dressing in the middle of the night. The audience must suspect that The Woman is Willy's mistress, with whom he just finished making love in this hotel room. When Willy says he's lonely, The Woman – a secretary at a company that Willy sells to – tries to cheer and console him by telling him that from now on she will send him right through to see the buyers without delay. Willy then tries to pull himself out of his depression by kissing The Woman after she only somewhat jokingly teases him about being sad and self-centered. Willy tries to ignore someone knocking at the door,

but finally opens it after making The Woman hide in the bathroom.

Willy discovers the young Biff at the door, extremely upset over flunking math. Biff asks Willy to persuade his math teacher to let Biff graduate: "[I]f he saw the kind of man you are, and you just talked to him in your way, I'm sure he'd come through for me.... He'd like you, Pop. You know the way you could talk." Willy agrees – partially as a way to keep Biff from entering the room and discovering The Woman – but Biff keeps talking. When Biff recounts how he once mocked the teacher, Willy laughs, but so does The Woman, unseen in the bathroom. Discovered, The Woman emerges from the bathroom, and Willy lies to Biff, explaining that she is simply "Miss Francis," a buyer whom he allowed to take a shower in his room while the hotel paints hers. Biff stares open-mouthed and horrified at her, realizing that his father has been cheating on his mother, Linda. Willy hurries The Woman out the door, but not before she demands the silk stockings Willy promised her.

Alone with Biff, Willy assures a weeping Biff that The Woman is merely a business associate. However, Biff clearly senses the truth and even Willy's promising to fix the flunking grade cannot win back Biff. Biff no longer believes the teacher would listen to Willy. Willy finally admits his infidelity: "She's nothing to me, Biff. I was lonely, I was terribly lonely." Biff will accept no explanation or excuse; seeing The Woman receive stockings that should have been his mother's, Biff rushes out of the room, weeping and yelling at Willy, "You fake! You phony little fake! You fake!"

As Biff leaves, Stanley enters, indicating to the audience that the flashback has ended and Willy remains in the restaurant. In a move of bravado, Willy tries to force a large tip on Stanley even though Biff and Hap have already paid the bill and tip. Stanley slips the money back into Willy's pocket when Willy is not looking; this gesture of common decency toward someone showing poor judgment contrasts Stanley with Willy and the other Loman men, who think nothing of lying and stealing. Learning from Stanley that his sons have left without him, Willy leaves to find seeds at a hardware store. It is late at night, as he exits, remarking anxiously, "I've got to get some seeds, right away. Nothing's planted. I don't have a thing in the ground."

The scene shifts back to the Loman house, where Biff and Hap enter late at night, finding Linda outraged at them for abandoning Willy at the restaurant. Anticipating Linda's anger, Hap has brought roses to calm her; he proceeds to pretend Willy had a terrific time tonight with them. Still enraged, Linda violently asks Biff whether he cares if Willy lives or dies. "Get out of here," Linda orders, "both of you, and don't come back!" Hap goes upstairs after Biff yells at him to stop pretending Willy spent a great evening with them. Biff had tried to deny Linda's accusations at first, but now he feels guilty and self-hating, calling himself the "scum of the earth." With determination – but still clearly ashamed of himself – Biff declares, "I gotta talk to the boss, Mom. Where is he?" A hammering noise is heard, and although Linda desperately wants Biff to leave Willy alone, she replies that Willy is in the yard planting a garden. Alarmed that Willy would plant a garden in the middle of the night, Biff goes outside, followed by Linda.

### Analysis

In this crucial section of the play, we plainly see that Willy has had an affair with a woman in Boston during his sales trips. Miller may refer to her as simply "The Woman" for a number of reasons; her lack of a name may indicate the way Willy does not really love but merely uses her to satisfy his sexual desire and to soothe his loneliness. Similarly, her giddy, laughing behavior contrasts sharply with Linda's warm, sensitive loyalty. By calling her "The Woman," Miller almost suggests she is ghostlike, a memory that has haunted Willy's guilty conscience for many years. Her appearing in silhouette in Act I, Part 3 and laughing unseen in Act II, Part 4 also lend her a ghostlike quality.

A "proper" woman of Willy's age, this woman does not strike us as someone whom Willy has chosen merely for her looks. More likely, her attraction to him flatters his pride, allowing him to feel "well liked," which has always been so important to him. Willy's contention that "she means nothing to me" may possibly be true, but neither Biff nor we can know for sure. Moreover, cheating on Linda without loving The Woman would simply signify the great extent of Willy's selfishness. While Willy may feel lonely on sales trips, Linda must suffer the same loneliness at home; she, though, is not unfaithful to Willy.

When Biff discovers Willy's affair, we understand that Biff's anger with Willy over the last 17 years stems from his knowledge of Willy's dishonesty. Rather than reveal Willy's infidelity to anyone, Biff has remained silent and held a grudge against his father. As we know from Act I, Part 4, Willy threw Biff out of the house because Biff knew he was a "fake." Although Biff never explained his reasons for calling his father a fake and phony, we now recognize Willy's affair as the source of Biff's hostility. Biff's discovery has a ripple effect: after discovering the affair, Biff dismisses his father's chances of convincing the math teacher to let Biff graduate. Biff now sees Willy's entire personality as a sham. Once the loyal son who took pride in his father's self-confidence, Biff feels disgusted at the salesman's arrogance and hollowness. Biff probably did, as Willy has suspected, decide not to attend summer school and graduate as a way of hurting, or spiting, Willy. Nevertheless, Biff may have deliberately or indeliberately never pursued a career with any true seriousness because he feared becoming "fake" like Willy. Nevertheless, it is clear that Willy would rather accuse Biff of spiting him than take responsibility for his own actions and their effects on his young son when he visited him in Boston.

Linda's anger with Biff and Hap recalls her desperation in Act I, Part 4. Apparently she has never learned of the affair. Linda's love of Willy requires that she defend Willy. Biff and Hap's insensitive behavior, she fears, will push Willy closer to despair and suicide. We do not know if Willy has told her he has been fired, but she already seems to know that she must keep Willy's hopes high – not to preserve any myth of future success but merely to keep Willy from killing himself. Because she loves him, she cannot abandon Willy – as Biff and Hap are ready to do. Although Linda does not strike us as a "fake," her life has depended heavily on seeing Willy not as a phony but simply a weary, well-meaning man; admitting or discovering he is a fake could throw her own sense of herself into complete confusion.

A strange resolve or sense of determination accompanies Biff's willingness to call himself the "scum of the earth." Hap may have cheered him up after leaving the restaurant, but now Biff succumbs again to the self-hate we saw him express to Willy in the restaurant. We cannot know why Biff wants to see Willy now, but we do know that Biff is once again more upset with himself than with Willy. For Biff, planting a garden at night signals another aspect of Willy's loss of sense and control. Planting evidently signifies some sort of necessity for Willy; he must plant soon not because cold weather will come soon, but because he must apparently *prepare* for something, though we cannot know what.

### Study Questions

1. Who is The Woman?

2. Approximately what age is Biff when he visits Willy in Boston?

3. What event causes Biff to come to Boston to see Willy?

4. What favor does Biff ask Willy to do?

5. What gift does The Woman insist that Willy give her before she will leave his room?

6. How does Willy initially explain the presence of The Woman in his room?

7. What is Biff's reaction to finding The Woman in his father's room? What does he yell at Willy as he leaves the room?

8. Why is Linda angry with Biff and Hap when they return to the house?

9. What does Linda order Biff and Hap to do? How does Biff respond?

10. Where is Willy at the end of this section? What is he doing?

### Answers

1. She is the woman with whom Willy has an affair during his sales trips to Boston. At one point he calls her "Miss Francis," but we cannot be sure this is her real name.

2. Biff is a senior in high school (about 17 or 18 years old). Most importantly, this is the *young* Biff, not the adult Biff who is in the restaurant as the Boston flashback begins.

3. Biff comes to Boston to find Willy after flunking math, which will prevent him from graduating high school.

4. Biff asks Willy to convince his math teacher not to flunk him, thus allowing him to graduate.

5. She insists Willy give her the stockings he promised her.

6. Willy lies to Biff, explaining The Woman's presence by saying that she is simply "Miss Francis," a buyer whom he allowed to take a shower in his room while the hotel paints hers.

7. Biff is horrified at his father's infidelity, losing all admiration for Willy. Weeping and rushing from the room, Biff yells, "You fake! You phony little fake! You fake!"

8. She is outraged that they abandoned Willy in the restaurant. She thinks such insensitivity may drive Willy closer to suicide.

9. Linda orders Biff and Hap to leave the house and never come back. Biff had tried to deny Linda's accusations at first, but he then begins to feel guilty and self-hating, calling himself the "scum of the earth."

10. Willy is in the yard, planting a garden in the middle of the night.

### Suggested Essay Topics

1. Discuss why Biff considers Willy a "fake." Try to show how Biff's discovery of Willy's affair causes Biff to lose trust in his father's character. Suggest the way in which Willy's dishonesty here finally opens Biff's eyes to the hollowness of Willy's strategies for success and being well liked. Biff now sees, for example, how his teacher will not listen to Willy because Willy is not the kind of man Biff previously thought him to be.

2. Write a paper in which you examine why Biff would feel guilty and self-hating. In this section, we learn he has reason to be disappointed in his father, so why does he continually condemn himself by calling himself something like the "scum of the earth"? The key to explaining Biff's self-hate may lie in his fear that he cannot live up to the expectations of success he set for himself when he was young; he fears

that he is a fake, like Willy. At the same time, Biff's self-hate seems to come also from his guilt over his own desire to abandon Willy and thereby abandon his mother, too.

# Act II, Part 6

*Summary*

Part 6 covers the action up to the end of Act II.

After Biff leaves the house with Linda, we see Willy alone on stage. Blue light covers the stage, indicating night time. With a flashlight, a hoe, and several packets of seeds, Willy begins to plant his garden. Ben appears and listens to Willy describe his "proposition," one that would leave $20,000 to Linda, who Willy says has suffered. (Today, that $20,000 would be equivalent to roughly $250,000.) The "proposition" implied is Willy's suicide, which would leave Linda the large amount of insurance money. Ben warns Willy that the insurance company might not pay if Willy's death were a suicide, but Willy remains confident that Linda would receive the money because he worked hard for years to meet the insurance payments.

Ben suggests that the proposition is also a cowardly solution to Willy's problems; however, Ben does agree with Willy that $20,000 is a significant amount of money. Willy adds that actual money is better than an appointment, implying that mere "appointments" cannot ensure success. Encouraged by Ben's response, Willy describes how a large funeral attended by all of Willy's business friends would impress Biff and win his sympathy: "Because he thinks I'm nothing, see, and so he spites me. But the funeral – Ben, that funeral will be massive!" When Ben replies that Biff will consider Willy a coward, Willy becomes worried again: "Why, why can't I give him something and not have him hate me?"

Ben drifts offstage as Biff appears. Biff tells Willy he wants to say good-bye because he has decided to leave and not return. Willy refuses to go inside the house with Biff because he does not wish to see Linda, but he then quickly enters the house when Biff con-

fesses, "This isn't your fault; it's me, I'm a bum." Inside the house Linda and, eventually, Hap are also present. Willy becomes angry when Biff insists he has no real appointment with Bill Oliver tomorrow. Willy refuses to take the blame for any future regret Biff will feel for ruining his own life merely to spite Willy. Biff becomes furious that Willy believes he is acting out of spite. Biff pulls out the rubber pipe, calls Willy a phony, and promises no pity for him if Willy commits suicide. Caught, Willy must listen as Biff attributes his own failures largely to Willy: "I never got anywhere because you blew me so full of hot air I could never stand taking orders from anybody!"

After stealing Oliver's pen, Biff explains, he realized that pursuing success through a business career was making him into someone he did not want to be. Refusing to accept Biff's idea that both of them are just ordinary, forgettable people, Willy bursts out, "I am Willy Loman, and you are Biff Loman!" Biff persists, "Pop, I'm nothing! I'm nothing, Pop. Can't you understand that? There's no spite in it any more. I'm just what I am, that's all…. Will you let me go, for Christ's sake? Will you take that phony dream and burn it before something happens?" Holding on to Willy, Biff begins to sob and then goes upstairs. Surprised by Biff's expression of affection, Willy's mood changes. Convinced that Biff does not actually spite him but likes him, Willy declares, "That boy – that boy is going to be magnificent!" Unnoticed by the Lomans, Ben replies, "Yes, outstanding, with twenty thousand dollars behind him."

Linda wants Willy to come to bed immediately, but he promises to come upstairs shortly. Alone with Ben again, Willy marvels at how Biff has always loved him and will "worship" him after receiving the $20,000. The money will even put Biff "ahead of Bernard again," Willy tells Ben; Ben agrees, calling it "a perfect proposition all around." Outside the house, now, Willy looks back and begins speaking as if he were once again giving Biff football advice and reminding him of the important people who would be watching the game.

Suddenly unable to find Ben, Willy becomes visibly nervous. Linda fearfully calls his name from inside the house; we see Biff and Hap listen for an answer. Willy rushes off the stage and soon a car is heard starting and speeding away. Music that has been get-

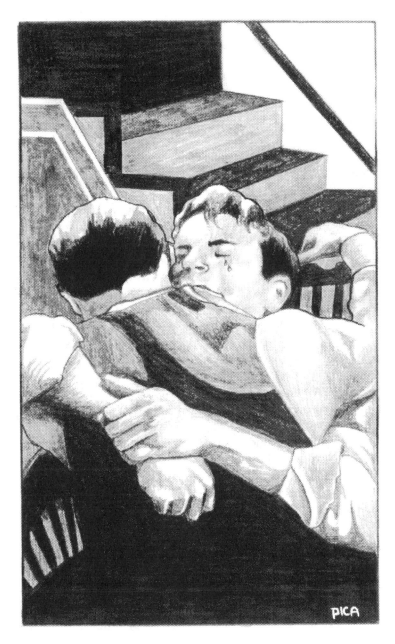

ting increasingly louder and more intense now crashes down and slow, sorrowful music begins. With sad expressions, Biff and Hap dress and descend to the kitchen. Charley and the adult Bernard enter. Linda enters from the living room in dark clothes of mourning, carrying a bunch of roses. The "leaves of day" appear, suggesting the passage of time. Moving through the wall-line of the kitchen, the characters leave the house and stand in front of a grave. Linda kneels.

### Analysis

In this section of the play, the seeds Willy plants are equated with the $20,000 he intends to give his family by committing suicide. Both the seeds and the money should bring a harvest in the future; the seeds will become full grown vegetables and the money will enable Linda and Biff to live respectable, comfortable lives. Willy is certain that the insurance company will pay, but we must doubt that it actually will; Willy's certainty strikes us as simply one more example of his wishful thinking and his failure to honestly face the facts of his life. He may have worked hard to pay for the insurance policy, but he should know by now that businesses – even insurance companies – rarely make decisions based on emotions such as loyalty. More importantly, perhaps, loyalty would not be extended to someone who has purposely attempted fraud.

Willy thinks a large, fancy funeral – like Dave Singleman's – will impress Biff, but when Biff confronts Willy with the rubber pipe, we see that Biff may indeed consider Willy a coward for killing himself. Biff expresses his rage over the "hot air" and phoniness that made him a dissatisfied, fake person. Clearly, Biff *does* feel disgust for Willy, but his decision to leave the house does not appear designed to spite Willy. Biff blames Willy for many of his (Biff's) failures, but Biff also accepts responsibility for them. Willy's affair with the Boston woman may have been the specific event that originally alerted Biff to Willy's dishonesty and arrogance, but Biff does not mention that revelation now, even though it has certainly had a deeply demoralizing and defeating effect on Biff's outlook and self-regard. Additionally, Biff may refrain from reference to the affair out of respect for his mother's feelings. Biff may have intentionally or unintentionally offended Willy by not pursuing summer school or a business career, but Biff's failure in all aspects of life has definitely not been deliberate and should not be considered a way of spiting Willy. Biff's disappointment in Willy and in himself stems from a whole life of conceit, self-deception, and defeat.

Although Willy has become frustrated with the empty promise of "appointments," he still attempts to maintain the fiction that Biff has an appointment with Bill Oliver. When Biff begins to cry, Willy finally perceives Biff's love for him. However, that perception only causes Willy to return to his old, misguided optimism: "That boy – that boy is going to be magnificent!" Furthermore, Willy's confidence that Biff will "worship" him once the insurance money arrives restores his selfish sense of competition: Biff will soon move "ahead of Bernard again." We realize Willy has not understood Biff's message; Willy continues to blow hot air, especially when he begins talking about football and the need to impress important people.

In this section of the play, Ben eventually encourages Willy to kill himself, calling it "a perfect proposition all around." Willy imagines Ben's presence merely to receive approval to kill himself. If Willy can believe that the older and supposedly wiser Ben would approve of the "proposition," then Willy can carry it out. Ben's presence assures Willy that $20,000 really represents something more dependable than anything else he can give his family. In addition to doubting that the money will be paid or that suicide will earn Biff's respect, we must wonder if there will be enough money to take care of both Linda and Biff. One moment Willy wants to give the money to Linda, and the next moment he wants to give it to Biff. Although $20,000 was worth much more in the 1940s than it is today, we cannot help but wonder if it would run out, leaving Linda and Biff where they were before Willy died.

The loud music that crashes down signals Willy's death: he has intentionally crashed his car. Willy probably chose to crash the car rather than breathe gas from the heater in the hope that the insurance company would consider the crash an accident and still pay the $20,000. However, Linda previously stated that the insurance company already suspected Willy of trying to kill himself; therefore, we know there is little possibility the insurance will honor the policy and pay. According to Willy's own conception of strong, brave manhood, suicide may indeed be a cowardly act. However, if we consider Willy as someone who has become truly confused and overwhelmed, then we may have some pity or sympathy for him, as Linda did when she called him "a little boat looking for a harbor."

Even though suicide may be a way of cowardly quitting, Willy's assertion that "I am Willy Loman, and you are Biff Loman!" reveals an admirable refusal to believe he is an insignificant person, a failure, a nobody. If we decide not to hate Willy or think of him as a fool, then we must somehow recognize the value of his sense of hope and belief in himself. Arthur Miller has described Willy's death as the tragedy of a common man, implying that Willy is a victim of his own stubborn desire to be loved as well as a victim of larger forces beyond his control. It becomes difficult to value Willy's hope and self-confidence when we see how they contributed to his death; however, it becomes somewhat less difficult when we know that his misguided belief in himself originally comes from a tendency in American culture sometimes to value superficial "personality" over hard work and integrity. While people like Charley and Bernard have earned the benefits of honest, hard work, Willy has suffered from his own self-deception as well as from the competitive business practices that finally care very little for individuals.

The end of this scene – which is the end of Act II – moves smoothly into the short final scene Miller calls the "Requiem." Willy's car crashes, but instead of leaving the house to find the accident, everyone slowly leaves the house – moving through the wall-line to indicate the passage of time – to attend Willy's funeral; clearly, a few days have passed between the crash and when Linda kneels in front of Willy's grave.

### Study Questions

1.  What is Willy's "proposition"?

2.  What effect does Willy think his death will have on Linda and Biff?

3.  Will the insurance company pay if it determines that Willy's death is a suicide rather than an accident?

4.  What is Biff's solution to ending the conflict between him and his father?

5.  What object does Biff show Willy?

6.  Has Biff spited Willy?

7.  Does Ben approve of Willy's "proposition"?

8.  What effect does Willy anticipate his death having on the continuing competition he imagines between Bernard and Biff?

9.  By the end of the scene, is Willy still angry with Biff?

10. How does Willy kill himself? What does the audience see or hear that reveals Willy's death?

### Answers

1.  His "proposition" refers to his plan to kill himself in order to leave Linda and Biff with $20,000 of insurance money.

2.  He believes his suicide will benefit rather than hurt Linda and Biff. Willy believes his death will end Linda's suffering because the insurance money will provide her with a comfortable life that Willy has not been able to give her. He thinks his death will also give Biff money with which to start a new life, causing Biff to "worship" Willy; furthermore, Willy thinks a well-attended funeral will impress Biff. Willy momentarily fears his suicide will cause Biff to consider him a coward, but then disregards this possibility.

3.  No. The insurance company will not pay the $20,000 if it knows Willy purposely killed himself. However, Willy cannot believe – after many years of his hard work – that the company would actually deny his family the money; he is probably wrong.

4.  He decides the best solution to their disagreements is for him simply to say good-bye and leave the family forever.

5.  Biff shows Willy the rubber pipe that Willy considered using to commit suicide.

6.  Biff says that spite has nothing to do with his frustration at Willy; he only wants to tell the truth about Willy's "hot air." However, we cannot disregard the way some of Biff's actions (not attending summer school, for example) may have indeed been intended to anger Willy.

7.  At first Ben does not give his approval, but eventually he does, calling Willy's plan a "perfect proposition all around."

8.  Willy believes that the insurance money from his death will put Biff "ahead of Bernard again." Willy still unnecessarily sees Biff and Bernard as competing for success. Willy's jealousy of Bernard's success fuels his desire to see Biff surpass Bernard.

9.  No. When Biff says, "There's no spite in it anymore" and then begins to cry, Willy sees that Biff likes him. Suddenly Willy's confidence in Biff returns: "That boy – that boy is going to be magnificent."

10. Willy kills himself by purposely crashing his car. The audience learns this by hearing the sounds of a car pulling away from the house. The crash of the loud music represents the car crashing. We know Willy has died when the slow music starts and we see Linda, Biff, Hap, Charley, and Bernard dressed somberly, standing by a grave.

### Suggested Essay Topics

1.  Write a paper in which you describe why Willy believes committing suicide will provide a better life for his family. Also discuss why his plan to kill himself may not result in the wonderful resolution of all the problems that have troubled him and his family.

2.  Analyze to what extent Willy is responsible for Biff's difficulties in life. What does Biff mean when he says, "I never got anywhere because you blew me so full of hot air I could never stand taking orders from anybody!" Can you find examples of Willy's "hot air" in this section of the play and elsewhere?

# *Requiem*

**Summary**

   The play's action flows smoothly from Willy's crash to his funeral. In the "Requiem" scene, we see Linda, Biff, Hap, Charley, and
Bernard gathered at Willy's grave. Hap, very angry, contends that
Willy had no right to kill himself, especially when Hap and Biff
would have helped him through his difficulties. Linda, kneeling in
front of the grave, wonders why no one has attended Willy's funeral: "But where are all the people he knew? Maybe they blame
him." Charley comforts her, telling her no one should blame Willy
for being who he was – a salesman. A salesman, Charley maintains,
is someone who dreams: "He's a man way out there in the blue,
riding on a smile and a shoeshine. And when they start not smiling back – that's an earthquake."

   Biff points out the way Willy actually put more feeling into his
carpentry and home repair work than he put into his sales. Biff,
therefore, disagrees with Charley: "Charley, the man didn't know
who he was." Furious that Biff would say such a thing, Hap pledges
to "show you and everybody else that Willy Loman did not die in
vain. He had a good dream. It's the only dream you can have – to
come out number-one man." While Hap decides to stay in New
York and continue Willy's struggle, Biff plans to leave, telling Hap,
"I know who I am."

   The cemetery will close its gates soon, but Linda lingers a little
longer at Willy's grave, while the others stand in the background.
Speaking to Willy's grave, she says, "Forgive me, dear. I can't cry. I
don't know what it is, but I can't cry. I don't understand it. Why did

you ever do that? Help me, Willy, I can't cry.... I made the last payment on the house today. Today, dear. And there'll be nobody home. We're free and clear. We're free. We're free. We're free." By the time Linda finishes, she has begun to sob. Biff leads her away. The flute music ("Willy's music") associated with the flashbacks has begun. We see the towering apartment buildings surrounding the Loman house come into sharp focus. The play ends.

### Analysis

The word "requiem" usually refers to a religious service or musical composition to honor someone who has died. Here we listen to the different ways in which Willy's family and friends honor or remember him. While "requiem" implies an elaborate, formal honoring of the dead, Willy's funeral has been very plain and attended by no one except Linda, Biff, Hap, Charley, and Bernard. So even though these few people express respect and sympathy for Willy, the funeral and their tributes fall short of what we would usually expect in an event titled "Requiem." Unlike Dave Singleman's funeral – which drew hundreds of people – this funeral reflects Willy's lack of popularity, his failure to be truly "well liked." We must suspect that few people have come because few people really liked Willy, not because they "blame" him or could never forgive him for committing suicide.

Hap continues to hope and to dream. In a sense, he has become Willy, convinced that success is always within reach and that success means being better than other people, being "number one." We must wonder if one day Hap will fall apart like Willy did when his dream appeared unreachable or reachable only through death. Biff will obviously not make the same mistakes as Willy and Hap, since Biff knows who he is. Yet, despite Biff's determination not to be a "fake," it is difficult not to think that Biff has given up too easily. Has he decided never to dream, never even to try to succeed? Or, has he in fact intelligently rid himself of the phoniness that was preventing him from being happy, satisfied with a life not judged according to Willy's misguided standards for success?

Charley's description of a salesman as the "man way out there in the blue" makes Willy's life sound exciting, adventurous, even romantic. We recognize that Willy may also have thought of his life that way. However, we also remember the loneliness and disappointment that Willy experienced. In light of his frustration, perhaps Biff is right to suggest that Willy would have been better off if he had known "who he was" and had not believed unrealistically in the rewards of a salesman's life.

Linda's disbelief over the lack of friends at Willy's funeral reveals to us the way she believed Willy when he told her of his popularity as a salesman. Her confusion demonstrates that she has not fully recognized – or refuses to recognize – Willy's "phoniness." Nevertheless, her disappointment also expresses her conviction that Willy deserves respect because he tried bravely to succeed even though he was not "a great man" but only a "human being," "a little boat in search of a harbor." The fact that the last payment has been made on the house attests to Willy's perseverance; although he was not extremely successful, he did work to make the house payments, a sign of his consistency.

The end of the house payments should have been reason to celebrate. After many years struggling to pay bills, Willy and Linda were beginning to need less money. They were increasingly "free and clear" of the obligations that had troubled them most of their lives. Because their lives were improving, Linda cannot understand why Willy killed himself. Willy, however, killed himself for many reasons other than his difficulty paying bills. He had begun to see his life as a failure because he could not live up to his own image of success; losing his job – which he apparently never told Linda – was only one event among many that led to his decision to kill himself. Biff's failure and hostility, as well as Bernard and Charley's success, also contributed to Willy's conclusion that he was "worth more dead than alive." There is no indication, though, that the insurance company paid the $20,000 to Willy's family. Most likely, the company refused to pay because Willy's death was ruled a suicide, not an accident.

When Linda repeatedly sobs, "We're free," she acknowledges the sad irony that Willy has killed himself just when their lives might have begun to improve. Such "freedom" becomes less desirable if it requires the death of someone you love. Furthermore, Linda's words suggest the way in which Willy was never free but rather always somehow under the control of his own distorted dreams –

dreams of success fed by deceptive, misleading cultural myths of success. In another sense, Linda and the rest of the family are free from Willy, someone who often made their lives difficult. While they never wanted Willy to kill himself, his absence may let them view life in a new, clearer way. Finally, there is a crucial, tragic irony in Linda's words, since Willy, despite being a salesman, failed all his life to grasp that people are not measured and valued by their material success, but, in fact, are "free" – beings without price, to whom no monetary amount can be affixed. Even in his choice of death, and the fact that he wanted his suicide to leave his family a great deal of money, Willy Loman never grasped the concept that people are intrinsically "free and clear."

As the play ends, the flute music plays. That music recalls the Lomans' happier days, when they believed in the dream that has by now fallen apart. Thus the music contrasts noticeably with the apartment buildings that become increasingly threatening as the play closes. The imposing buildings – and the uncaring, anonymous way of business they seem to represent – have suffocated Willy, but we also sense that Willy should have recognized his own mistakes and arrogance. We receive the impression that Miller has not rejected Willy's optimism (the flute), but he wants to warn us about the dangers of naively following a dream or the perils of desperately wanting to be loved. While it is possible to consider Willy a victim, a coward, or a hero, it is the mixing of these three identities that makes any of them meaningful. Readers of *Death of a Salesman* sometimes disagree over how much sympathy Willy deserves. Some readers think Miller has created in Willy a character whose own selfishness is so great that we can find no salvageable, redeeming qualities in him. Even if some readers do not believe Willy deserves any sympathy, they should still be able to see where the play itself expresses sympathy for Willy.

### Study Questions

1. Do many people attended Willy's funeral?

2. What is Hap's mood? What does he plan to do?

3. According to Charley, to what should we attribute Willy's frustration and death?

4.  Where does Biff think Willy actually put his greatest feeling – into his job as a salesman or elsewhere?

5.  According to Biff, why did Willy live a life of misplaced hope, a life that ended in suicide?

6.  Will Biff stay in New York and pursue the career Willy hoped he would?

7.  Has Willy's family received the $20,000 that Willy thought the insurance company would pay them upon his death?

8.  Why does Linda find it hard to understand why Willy killed himself?

9.  What words does Linda repeat as the play ends?

10. What music lingers as the play ends? What becomes more prominent visually at the same time?

### *Answers*

1.  No. Unlike Dave Singleman's funeral, Willy's funeral is attended by very few people – only Linda, Biff, Hap, Charley, and Bernard.

2.  Hap is very angry with Willy for killing himself, but he plans to stay in New York and work to see Willy's dream come true.

3.  Charley thinks growing frustration from his lack of success as a salesman caused Willy's frustration and suicide; a salesman loses confidence when unliked, when customers no longer smile back.

4.  Biff points out the way Willy actually put more feeling into his carpentry and home repair work than he put into his sales.

5.  Biff believes that Willy "didn't know who he was." In other words, Willy pursued a life and career that did not correspond with his true feelings or abilities.

6.  No. "I know who I am," Biff asserts, distancing himself from Willy and Hap. Unlike Hap, Biff plans to leave New York, probably to return to the small, outdoor jobs he prefers over office work.

7. There is no indication that the insurance company paid the money. Most likely, the company refused to pay because Willy's death was ruled a suicide, not an accident.

8. Linda believes their lives had been improving before Willy's death, indicated by the fact that she has finally made the last house payment.

9. She sobs, "We're free and clear. We're free. We're free. We're free." She means she and Willy are now free and clear of house payments, but her words also express an ironic recognition that any freedom attained has somehow come at the cost of Willy's life. Her words also recognize the irony in Willy's inability to grasp the idea that people are not commodities of materialistic value but intrinsically "free."

10. The flute music identified with Willy's flashbacks of happier days begins to play as the apartment buildings surrounding the Loman house become increasingly visible and threatening.

### Suggested Essay Topics

1. Write a paper in which you explore the difference between Biff and Hap's reactions to Willy's death. Has Willy's death changed the way they viewed him before he committed suicide? Does Hap seem more upset in the "Requiem" section than he was in Act II? Does Biff not share Hap's anger over Willy's suicide or does he express it differently?

2. Write a paper in which you compare the outcome of Willy's death with the various ways Willy envisioned it earlier in the play. How does Willy's funeral compare with Dave Singleman's? Is Willy "worth more dead than alive," as he said to Charley? Has Willy's suicide turned out to be a "great proposition all around," as Ben thought?

# SECTION FIVE

# *Sample Analytical Paper Topics*

The following paper topics are based on the entire play. Following each topic is a thesis and sample outline. Use these as a starting point for your paper.

### Topic #1

*Death of a Salesman* encompasses two different moments in time, approximately 17 years apart. The scenes of the earlier period occur as flashbacks and may even be considered Willy's memories or hallucinations. Discuss the way those scenes reveal important information that allows us to understand characters' motivations.

### Outline

I.   Thesis Statement: *Arthur Miller uses the flashback scenes of the past to reveal the psychological motivations of the characters' actions in the present.*

II.  First Flashback(s): Biff and Happy as teenagers, and Willy, Linda, and The Woman

    A.   Why Willy's curtailed trip to New England has caused him to remember this flashback

    B.   Biff and Hap's conversation as adults compared with Biff and Hap as teenagers

    C.  Willy's enthusiasm and desire to be well liked and his present disappointment in Biff

    D.  Willy's affair with "The Woman" and its effect on his feelings for Linda

III.  Second Flashback(s): Willy and Ben

    A.  Willy's different reactions to Charley's job offers and Ben's job offer

    B.  Willy and Ben's similar but different philosophies of competition, success, and the "jungle" of life

    C.  Willy's attempts to impress Ben and win his approval, including approval to commit suicide

IV.  Third Flashback(s): Willy, "The Woman," and Biff in Boston

    A.  Explanations for why the restaurant meeting triggers Willy's memory of Biff's visit to Boston

    B.  The source of Biff's opinion of Willy as a "fake"

    C.  How the memory of the affair affects Willy's behavior toward Linda

V.  The role of sound, lighting, and set design in indicating the flashbacks and their significance

VI.  The effect of interspersing the flashbacks among the events in the present, 17 years later

VII.  Continuities and discontinuities between characters' behavior during the flashbacks and their behavior in the present

### Topic #2

Miller focuses considerable attention on Willy's occupation as a salesman. Discuss the importance of Miller's decision to use the figure of the salesman as the central character of his play.

### Outline

I.  Thesis Statement: *Being a salesman not only constitutes Willy's occupation but shapes his entire personality and outlook on life. His identity as a salesman greatly influences his attitudes*

> *toward his family and neighbors, as well as his decision to com-
> mit suicide.*

II.   The salesman's confidence

  A.   Examples of Willy's consistent belief in a better tomorrow

  B.   Willy's equation of "personality" with success

  C.   Competition and masculinity: Biff and Hap's childhood

  D.   The ideals of Dave Singleman and Ben

III.  Disillusion

  A.   The arrogance and selfishness of "personality"

  B.   "Business is business": the irrelevance of personality

  C.   "Selling" the truth: cheating and other secrets

  D.   Self-deception: Willy, Biff, and the consequences of
       "hot air"

IV.   The way in which the positive or harmless aspects of Willy's
      confidence as a salesman symbolize and express deeper, nega-
      tive, and harmful aspects of his character and emotional in-
      stability

V.    Placing blame: The various sources, including Willy himself,
      responsible for the failure and suffering that arise from Willy's
      conception of the "salesman"

### Topic #3

   Although Willy Loman is the main character of *Death of a Salesman*, Linda also plays a crucial role in the play. Look again at the
way Linda mediates between or balances Willy and his sons. Describe the various positions, attitudes, and beliefs she adopts as
she interacts with the other characters.

### Outline

I.    Thesis Statement: *Linda Loman represents a point of view that
      mediates the conflicting views of Willy and his sons. Not merely
      a kindhearted housewife, she struggles to keep her family to-
      gether.*

II.  Linda's loyalty as a housewife

    A.  Greeting Willy when he returns home early

    B.  Comforting Willy

    C.  Sending Willy off to work

III.  Linda asserts herself

    A.  Confronting Biff

    B.  Standing up to Willy and Ben

    C.  Telling Biff and Hap to leave the house

IV.  Linda's opinion of Willy

    A.  Recognizing Willy's faults

    B.  **Recognizing Willy's exhaustion, vulnerability, and humanity**

V.  To what degree do Linda's attempts to defend and protect Willy reveal her to share Willy's unrealistic sense of optimism?

VI.  Linda's reaction to Willy's death

# SECTION SIX

# *Bibliography*

Quotations of *Death of a Salesman* are taken from the following edition:

Miller, Arthur. *Death of a Salesman: Certain Private Conversations in Two Acts and a Requiem.* 1949. New York: Penguin Books, 1985.

The following works were also consulted during the course of this work:

Bloom, Harold, ed. *Arthur Miller: Modern Critical Views.* New York: Chelsea House Publishers, 1987.

Helterman, Jeffrey. "Arthur Miller." *Dictionary of Literary Biography, Vol. 7: Twentieth-Century American Dramatists.* John MacNicholas, ed. Detroit: Gale Research Company, 1981.

Koon, Helene Wickham, ed. *Twentieth Century Interpretations of* Death of a Salesman: *A Collection of Critical Essays.* Englewood Cliffs, NJ: Prentice-Hall, Inc., 1983.

Miller, Arthur. Death of a Salesman: *Text and Criticism.* Gerald Weales, ed. New York: Viking/Penguin, 1981.

——. *The Theater Essays of Arthur Miller.* Robert A. Martin, ed. New York: The Viking Press, 1978.

Moss, Leonard. *Arthur Miller.* Revised edition. Boston: Twayne Publishers, 1980.

Welland, Dennis. *Miller: The Playwright.* Revised edition. New York and London: Methuen, Inc., 1983.

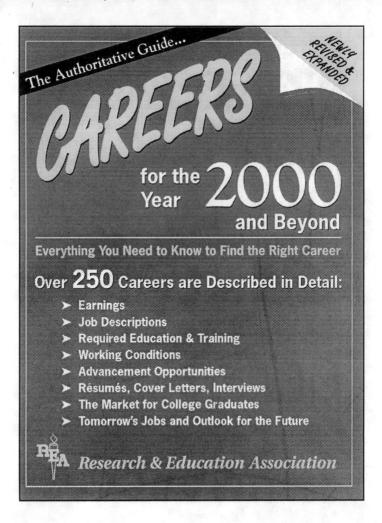